Mug Hugs

ALISON HOWARD

Mug Hugs

GUILD OF MASTER CRAFTSMAN PUBLICATIONS

First published in 2010 by
Guild of Master Craftsman Publications Ltd
Castle Place, 166 High Street,
Lewes, East Sussex BN7 1XU

ISBN 978-1-86108-690-7

A record of this book is available from the
British Library.

Charts and pattern checking by Gina Alton
Knitting illustrations by Simon Rodway

Associate Publisher: Jonathan Bailey
Production Manager: Jim Bulley
Managing Editor: Gerrie Purcell
Senior Project Editor: Dominique Page
Managing Art Editor: Gilda Pacitti
Designer: Ginny Zeal

Set in Gill Sans

Colour origination by GMC Reprographics
Printed and bound in Thailand by
Kyodo Nation Printing

Why we love mug hugs

THERE'S SOMETHING ABOUT PUTTING ON THE KETTLE that seems to tempt fate: just as you settle down to a nice, hot drink the telephone or the doorbell will ring, or some other crisis will rear its ugly head. Mug hugs are the perfect way to consign cold coffee or tepid tea to the dustbin of history.

Mug hugs do exactly what it says on the cover: they hug your mug to keep the contents lovely and warm. Make one in your favourite colour or to match your favourite teapot or cafetière cozy. Add a base, and you won't even need a separate coaster. They are an ideal way to use up odds and ends of yarn, and they make fabulous, quickly worked gifts. But watch out, because everybody will want one!

Contents

 9

 10

 11

 12

 13

 14

 15

 16

This design uses only garter stitch and is an ideal first project for new knitters. The fastenings are simple to work using only extra cast-on and cast-off stitches, but if you want to keep it really easy, just omit them.

Simply snug

Materials

Wool or wool-mix yarn (examples show Sirdar Escape Chunky in 192 Luscious and Twilleys Freedom Spirit DK in 518 Desire)

25g chunky yarn

A pair of 4.5mm (UK7:US7) needles

OR

20g DK yarn

A pair of 3.75mm (UK9:US5) needles

Darning needle for sewing up

2 medium buttons or 2 small toggles (optional)

Size

To fit a standard-height mug approx 4in (10cm) tall × any circumference**

**Measure round the outside of the mug, excluding handles*

Note: If your mug is taller than the standard size shown in these projects, you may prefer to cast on a few extra stitches. An extra 2 stitches (chunky) or 3 stitches (DK) will increase the depth by about ½in (1cm).

Tension

Chunky: 18 sts to 4in (10cm) in width measured over garter stitch on 4.5mm needles

DK: 22 sts to 4in (10cm) in width measured over garter stitch on 3.75mm needles

Special techniques

Casting on (see p.134)
Garter stitch (see p.138)
Casting off (see p.145)

Pattern notes

If you are really worried about making fastenings, don't bother! Garter stitch is very stretchy, so the hug will fit easily over the mug handle if it is simply sewn together at top and bottom.

To make a hug without fastenings, cast on 14 sts (chunky) or 18 sts (DK), leaving a long end. Knit a strip long enough to fit round mug and cast off all stitches, leaving a long end. Use long yarn ends to join the strip at top and lower edges (sew together one stitch at top and two stitches at lower edge). Decorate with buttons if preferred.

Method

Chunky yarn (button loops at each end of one side)
(See facing page)

Cast on 28 sts, leaving a long end.
Row 1: Cast off 14 sts (first button loop made), knit to end of row, turn.
Row 2: Cast on 14 sts, then cast them off immediately (second button loop made). Knit to end of row.
Row 3: Knit all sts.
Work in garter stitch until the strip is long enough to fit round the mug between the edges of the handle when slightly stretched. Remember that garter stitch is quite springy so don't stretch it too much.
Cast off, leaving a long end of yarn.

DK yarn (button loops top and centre) *(See page 11)*

Cast on 18 sts, leaving a long end. Work in garter stitch until the strip is long enough to fit round mug when slightly stretched.

Make button loops

Next row: Cast on 16 sts, then cast them off immediately (first loop made).

Turn work, pull yarn firmly to prevent a hole forming, then cast off another 8 sts down the side. Turn work again. Cast on another 16 sts, then cast them off immediately (second loop made). Turn work, pull yarn firmly, and cast off rem sts. Pull the yarn through the loop to fasten off, leaving a long end.

Making up

Chunky: Attach buttons or toggles to the cast-off end of the work. Fold the cast-on and cast-off ends of yarn back to make button loops and pin them in place. Try hug on mug to make sure loops are the correct length, and adjust if necessary. Sew button loops in place.

DK: Thread the darning needle using one end of yarn, join the last 2 stitches of cast-on and cast-off edges of work (this will be the bottom of the hug). Attach buttons or toggles to the cast-on edge, placing one at the top and one in the centre. Fold the cast-on and cast-off ends of loops back and pin in place. Try on the mug to make sure loops are the correct length, and adjust if necessary. Sew button loops in place.

This design is based on a simple rectangle of stocking stitch, worked sideways with narrow garter-stitch borders to stop it curling at the sides.
Use any DK yarn, or, for an extra-thick version, use the yarn double.

On the edge

Materials

Any standard DK yarn
A pair of 3.75mm (UK9:US5) needles
OR
Version A: Sirdar Luxury Cotton DK
Approx 20g in Liberty Blue
A pair of 4mm (UK8:US6) needles
Version B: Sirdar Wash 'n' Wear Crepe DK
Approx 25g in Flamenco (used double)
A pair of 4.5mm (UK7:US7) needles
Darning needle for sewing up
Button

Size

3¼in (8cm) deep × any circumference (adjustable)
Note: If your mug is taller than this, you may prefer to cast on a few extra stitches. An extra 2 stitches (chunky) or 3 stitches (DK used double/chunky) will increase the depth by about ½in (1cm).

Tension

Standard DK yarn: 24 sts to approx 4in (10cm) in width measured over stocking stitch on 3.75mm needles

Cotton (bulky) DK yarn: 22 sts to approx 4in (10cm) in width measured over stocking stitch on 4mm needles

DK used double/chunky yarn: 16 sts to approx 4in (10cm) in width measured over stocking stitch on 4.5mm needles

Special techniques

Garter stitch (see p.138)
Stocking stitch (see p.138)

Method

Version A: Blue (DK yarn)

Note: The yarn used for version A is thicker than standard DK, so fewer stitches are required. If using a standard DK yarn, follow the instructions in brackets.

Using 4mm needles, cast on 16[20] sts, leaving a long end of yarn.

Work 3 rows in garter stitch.

Next row: K2, p to last 2 sts, k2.

Next row: Knit all sts.

These two rows set the stocking stitch with a garter-stitch edge. Repeat them until the work is almost long enough to fit round mug when slightly stretched. Work 3 more rows in garter stitch.*

Make button loop

Cast off 14[18] sts, turn. 2 sts.

Next row: Knit these 2 sts.

Work in garter stitch on these 2 sts for approx 3in (7.5cm).

Cast off, leaving a long end.

Alternative button loop (1)

Work to *, then cast off all stitches leaving a long end.

Use the yarn end to crochet a chain loop approx 4in (10cm) long.

Alternative button loop (2)

Work to *, turn and cast on 16 sts.

Cast off these 16 sts immediately, and continue casting off to end.

Fasten off.

Version B: Red (two strands of DK)

Note: Standard chunky yarn can be substituted for DK yarn used double. Check tension carefully.

Using 4.5mm needles and two strands of DK yarn together, cast on 12 sts, leaving a long end.

Work 3 rows in garter stitch.

Next row: K1, p to last 2 sts, k1.

Next row: Knit all stitches.

These two rows set the stocking stitch with a garter-stitch edge. Repeat these rows until work is almost long enough to fit round the mug when slightly stretched.

Work 3 rows in garter stitch.*

Cast off 10 sts, turn. 2 sts.

Make button loop

Next row: Knit these 2 sts.
Work in garter stitch on these 2 sts
for approx 4in (10cm).
Cast off, leaving a long end.

Alternative button loop (1)

Cast off all sts at * and use the yarn
end to work a crochet chain loop
approx 4in (10cm) long.

Alternative button loop (2)

Cast on 14 sts at *, and cast them
off immediately. Cast off rem sts.
Fasten off.

Making up

Thread the darning needle using the
end of yarn left when casting on, and
join the first two stitches of the cast-on
edge to the corresponding stitches on
the cast-off edge. This will be the lower
edge of the mug hug. Slip the hug over
the mug. Fold back the button loop
and pin in place, adjusting as necessary.
Sew in place.

Tip

*For a simple decoration,
add a sew-on motif or
a badge to your hug.*

The easiest way to make simple knitting interesting is by adding stripes. Choose any colours you like and work either in garter stitch or stocking stitch with a garter-stitch border – instructions are given for both.

Stripes

Materials

Sublime Angora Merino 80% merino wool, 20% angora (131yd/120m per 50g ball)
Oddments in 044 Berry, 072 Giggle Pink and 047 Dusky
A pair of 3.75mm (UK9:US5) needles
Darning needle for sewing up
Button (optional)
Crochet hook (optional)

Size

3¼in (8cm) deep × any circumference (adjustable)

Tension

24 sts to 4in (10cm) in width measured over garter stitch on 3.75mm needles

Special techniques

Garter stitch (see p.138)
Stocking stitch (optional) (see p.138)
Chain stitch or blanket stitch (see pp.147–148) for optional button loop

Pattern notes

There is a right side to this design: the wrong side shows the loops that are produced whenever a different yarn is introduced. Make sure yarn ends are darned in on the wrong side. Garter stitch is very stretchy, so no fastening is necessary, but if you prefer to add a loop and button, instructions are given.

Method

Garter stitch (See page 19)

Cast on 18 sts, leaving a long end.
Work 3 rows in garter stitch (every row knit) before beginning stripes.
Work in garter stitch, changing colour every 2 or 4 rows to form a pleasing stripe pattern. Continue in pattern until work, when slightly stretched, is almost long enough to fit round the mug, ending with a WS row.
Work 3 rows in garter stitch, in a single colour, preferably that used to cast on.
Cast off, leaving a long end.

Stocking stitch (See facing page)

Cast on 18 sts, leaving a long end.
Work 3 rows in garter stitch before starting stripes.
Row 1: Knit to end.
Row 2: K2, p to last 2 sts, k2.
These two rows set the garter-stitch border. Repeat until work is almost long enough to fit round the mug when slightly stretched, ending on a WS row.
At the same time, change yarn colour every 2 or 4 rows to form a pleasing stripe pattern.
Note: When you change colour for stripes, work the left-hand garter-stitch edge with a small extra ball of yarn.
Using a single colour, work 3 rows in garter stitch.
Cast off, leaving a long end.

Making up

Thread the darning needle using one of the ends of yarn left when casting on, and join the first 2 stitches of the cast-on edge to the corresponding stitches on the cast-off edge. This will be the top of the mug. Thread the needle on the remaining end of yarn and join from the lower edge to just under the handle of the mug, checking the fit if necessary. Slip cover over mug.

Button loop (optional)

Using the yarn in the main shade used for the hug, insert a hook one-third of the way down the opening side and crochet a chain long enough to form a button loop. Slip stitch the chain into the cover exactly two-thirds of the way down and fasten off.
Note: If you cannot crochet, make a loop of yarn and finish it off using blanket stitch (see page 150).
Sew in ends. Attach button to hug to correspond with the loop.

There's no need to buy yarn to work this cheerful project – it's made from oddments of DK that are simply knotted together. Beg or borrow scraps, or use it as an excuse to clear out all the bits lurking in your workbox.

Bits and bobs

Materials
Patons Fairytale Colour 4 Me DK 100% wool
(98yd/90m per 50g)
Oddments in various shades
A pair of 3.75mm (UK9:US5) needles
Darning needle for sewing up

Size
3½in (9cm) deep x any circumference (adjustable)
Note: If your mug is taller than the example shown, cast on extra stitches to make the hug deeper. An extra 3 stitches will increase the depth by approx ½in (1cm).

Tension

5 sts to 1in (2.5cm) in width measured over garter stitch on 3.75mm needles

Special techniques

Garter stitch (see p.138)

Pattern notes

Before beginning to knit, gather a selection of yarns in approx DK weight and cut into lengths of at least 20in (50cm). Choose contrasting tones for dramatic effect or complementary tones for a more muted effect (see examples). Vary the lengths of yarn so the stripes are not too regular and the knots do not appear in the same place on each row. To join lengths, place two cut ends of yarn together and form a loop to knot them neatly and firmly. Wind the knotted yarn into a ball.

Method

Cast on 18 sts, leaving a long end for sewing up.

Work in garter stitch, pushing the knots through to the front as you go, and adjusting if necessary, to ensure that they do not poke through too close to the edges of your work.

Continue until work is long enough to fit round mug when slightly stretched. Cast off, leaving a long end.

Making up

Thread the darning needle using the end of yarn left when casting on, and join the first stitch of the cast-on edge to the corresponding stitch on the cast-off edge. This will be the top of the hug. Using the remaining end of yarn, join from the lower edge of the hug to just under the handle of the mug, checking the fit if necessary. Slip the hug over the mug and stroke the knots downwards to produce the desired effect.

This design was inspired by a pure wool variegated yarn in lovely shades of green, so it was easy to decide which stitch to use. Moss stitch is easy to work and produces a firm, dense fabric that is ideal for keeping drinks hot.

Moss

Materials

Twilleys Freedom Spirit DK 100% wool
(131yd/120m per 50g)
Approx 25g in 514 Nature
A pair of 3.75mm (UK9:US5) needles
Darning needle for sewing up
Button
Crochet hook (optional) for alternative button loop

Size

3¼in (8cm) deep x any circumference (adjustable)
Note: If your mug is taller than the example used, cast on extra stitches to make the hug deeper. Make sure you cast on an even number of stitches, and work extra stitches into the pattern. An extra 6 stitches will increase the depth by just over 1in (2.5cm).

Tension

5.5 sts to 1in (2.5cm) in width
measured over moss stitch
on 3.75mm needles

Special techniques

Moss stitch (see p.138)

Method

Cast on 18 sts, leaving a long end
for sewing up.

Pattern row: (k1, p1); rep to end.
This row forms moss stitch pattern.
Continue in pattern until the work
is almost long enough to fit round
the mug when slightly stretched.*

Make button loop

Next row: Cast on 16 sts at
beg of next row, then cast them
off immediately.

Cast off rem sts and fasten off, leaving
a long end.

Alternative button loop

Work cover to *, then cast off all sts, leaving a long end.
Use yarn end to crochet a chain loop for button.

Making up

Thread darning needle using the end of yarn left when casting on, and use to join the first two stitches of the cast-on edge to the corresponding stitches on the cast-off edge. This will be the lower edge of the hug.

Attach button to the top edge of the hug, opposite loop. Place hug on mug, fold back loop and pin in place. Check fit, then thread the darning needle on remaining end of yarn and sew in place.

This easy block design is worked using only garter stitch with simple increases and decreases. It will fit almost any mug and may be fastened on either side, so it's perfect for a left-hander.

Fits any size

Materials

Any chunky alpaca yarn (approx 98yd/90m per 50g)

Approx 35g in Off-white

A pair of 4mm (UK8:US6) needles

3 buttons

Size

To fit any size mug (adjustable)

Tension

5 sts to 1in (2.5cm) in width measured over garter stitch on 4mm needles

Special techniques

Making a buttonhole (see method)
Increasing (inc1): Work into the front, then the back of the stitch
Decreasing: Skpo (right-slanting) or k2tog (left-slanting)
Skpo: Slip 1 st, knit 1 st, pass slipped stitch over

Pattern notes

If you really don't think you can manage to make a buttonhole, don't make one! Just work a tab in plain garter stitch, omitting the buttonhole, then sew the first button to the front of the tab and add a press fastener to the back. Alternatively, just use a pretty pin, badge or brooch to fasten the hug.

Method

Cast on 7 sts.
Row 1: (WS): Knit.
Row 2: Inc1, knit to last st, inc1. 9 sts.
Row 3: Knit.
Row 4: Inc1, knit to last st, inc1. 11 sts.
Row 5: Knit.
Row 6 (first buttonhole row): K4, cast off 3 sts knit-wise, k4.
Row 7 (second buttonhole row): K4, cast on 3 sts over sts of previous row, k4.

Row 8: K4, k3 cast-on sts, k4.

Rows 9–13: Knit.

Row 14: Inc1, knit to last st, Inc1. 13 sts.

Row 15: Knit.

Rep last 2 rows twice. 17 sts.

Work in garter stitch (every row knit) until the straight piece of the work is long enough to reach round the mug between the edges of the handle, ending with a WS row.

Next row: Skpo, k to last 2 sts, k2tog.

Next row: Knit.

Rep last 2 rows until there are 11 sts on needle.

Cast off.

Making up

Sew on the three buttons as shown.

Darn in yarn ends.

Tip

Remember that the buttons do not have to match – this project is an ideal way to use up odd ones.

This wacky design looks complicated but it's actually really easy: all it takes is casting on, casting off and garter stitch. The fine alpaca yarn is used double to produce a really warm, thick fabric.

Tiny tags

Materials

Artesano Inca Cloud 100% alpaca (131yd/120m per 50g)

Approx 35g in 508 Lilac

A pair of 4mm (UK8:US6) needles

Button or toggle

Darning needle for sewing up

Size

3¼in (8cm) deep x any circumference (adjustable)

Tension

Not critical as work is stretchy

Special techniques

Making a buttonhole (see instructions)
Increasing (inc1): Knit into the front,
then the back of the next st
Skpo: Slip 1 st, knit 1 st, pass slipped
stitch over
Garter stitch (see p.138)

Pattern notes

If you are feeling really ambitious, you
can work the tags in contrast yarn,
carrying the yarn loosely across the
back of the work on each 'tag' row.
Remember that this will mean lots of
extra yarn ends to sew in! For a really
'punk' look, which looks particularly
good in black yarn, work longer tags by
casting on/off 4, 5, or even 6 stitches
for each tag. If you do not want to
work a buttonhole, just work plain
garter stitch tabs and use a pretty pin
or badge to fasten the hug.

Method

Using yarn double, cast on 7 sts.

First tab

Knit 1 row.

Row 2: Inc1, knit to end. 8 sts.
Row 3: Inc 1, knit to end. 9 sts.
Row 4: Inc1, knit to end. 10 sts.
Row 5 (first buttonhole row): Inc1,
k2, cast off 3 sts, knit to end.

Row 6 (second buttonhole row):
Inc1, k3, cast on 3 sts over cast-off sts
of previous row, k4. 12 sts.
Row 7: Inc1, k to end. 13 sts.
Row 8: Inc1, k to last st, inc1. 15 sts.
Row 9: Inc1, k to last st, inc1. 17 sts.
Now work in pattern:

Tag pattern

Row 1: Knit.
Row 2: Purl.
Row 3 (RS): K3, insert needle in next st
and cast 3 sts on to left needle; cast off
these 3 sts immediately (1 tag worked);
k3, work tag, k3, work tag, k3, work tag, k1
(4 tags worked).
Rows 4, 5 and 6: Knit.
Row 7: K1, (work tag, k3) to end.
Row 8: Knit.
These 8 rows set the pattern,
producing 4 tags on each row.
Rep until pattern section is long
enough to reach round circumference
of mug between edges of handle.
Now work in garter stitch only to
shape tab.

Second tab

Next row: Skpo, k to last 2 sts, k2tog.
15 sts.
Next row: Knit.
Next row: Skpo, k to last 2 sts, k2tog.
13 sts.
Knit 3 rows.
Next row: Skpo, k to last 2 sts, k2tog.
11 sts.
Next row: Knit.

Next row: Skpo, k to last 2 sts, k2tog.
9 sts.
Cast off.

Making up

Sew on button. Darn in yarn ends.

> ## Tip
> *If a tag falls where you
> want to place the button, just push
> it through to the reverse of the work
> and sew it down neatly.*

This design is worked sideways, with a central pattern panel and garter-stitch edges, and fastened by a knitted-in button loop. The pure wool Shetland yarn used is just the same shade as milky coffee.

Frothy coffee

Materials

Pure wool Aran-weight Shetland yarn
Approx 20g in Coffee
A pair of 4mm (UK8:US6) needles
Darning needle for sewing up

Size

To fit a standard-height mug approx 4in (10cm) tall
3in (8cm) tall × any circumference**
**Measure round the outside of the mug, excluding handle
Note: If your mug is taller than the standard mug shown, cast on an even number of extra stitches to make the hug deeper and work them into the garter-stitch borders.

Tension

20 sts to 4in (10cm) in width measured over pattern on 4mm needles
Check tension carefully

Special techniques

P2togtbl: Purl 2 sts together into the back loops of the stitches
Skpo: Slip 1 st, knit 1 st, pass slipped stitch over

Method

Cast on 15 sts, leaving a long end of yarn for sewing up.
Knit 2 rows.
Beg patt:
Row 1 (WS): K3, p9, k3.
Row 2: K2, p1, yo, k4, skpo, k3, p1, k2.
Row 3: K3, p2, p2togtbl, p4, yo, p1, k3.
Row 4: K2, p1, k2, yo, k4, skpo, k1, p1, k2.
Row 5: K3, p2togtbl, p4, yo, p3, k3.
Row 6: K2, p1, k9, p1, k2.
Row 7: K3, yo, p4, p2tog, p3, k3.
Row 8: K2, p1, k2, k2tog, k4, yo, k1, p1, k2.
Row 9: K3, p2, yo, p4, p2tog, p1, k3.
Row 10: K2, p1, k2tog, k4, yo, k3, p1, k2.
These 10 rows form the patt.
Rep them until work is almost long enough to reach round mug when slightly stretched, excluding handle.
Knit 2 rows.

Make button loop

Next row: Cast on 18 sts, then cast

them off immediately. Cont casting off to last 3 sts (including st on needle). Work in garter stitch on these 3 sts for approx 4in (10cm) or length required for button loop.
Cast off, leaving a long end of yarn.

Making up

Press lightly, following instructions on ball band. Thread the darning needle using the end of yarn left when casting on and use to join the first 2 or 3 stitches of the garter-stitch border to the corresponding stitches on the other side. This will be the bottom of the hug. Darn in the yarn end. Attach the button to the top of the hug opposite the button loop. Try it on the mug, and pin the loop in place with the free end 2 stitches below beg of loop. Now thread the other length of yarn on the darning needle and sew the loop firmly in place. Make sure that the loop is long enough to fit over the handle without stretching the work.

This two-colour woven pattern may look complicated, but it is really easy
once you have mastered it. For a different effect vary the shades used:
oatmeal and brown work well, and black and white are striking.

Waffle weave

Materials

Paton's Fairytale Colour 4 Me DK 100% wool
(98yd/90m per 50g)
Approx 20g in 4954 Blueberry (A)
Approx 20g in 4952 Lime green (B)
A pair of 4mm needles (UK8:US6)
Darning needle for sewing up
Button

Size

3¼in (8cm) tall x any circumference (adjustable)
*Note: If your mug is taller than the one shown, cast on extra
stitches to make the hug deeper. Make sure the number of
cast-on stitches is divisible by 2, and work extra stitches into
the pattern. An extra 3 stitches will increase the depth by
about ½in (1cm).*

Tension

24 sts to 4in (10cm) in width measured over pattern using 4mm needles

Special techniques

Sl1wyb: Slip one stitch with the yarn held at the back of work

Sl1wyf: Slip one stitch with the yarn held at the front of work

Pattern notes

For best results use the recommended yarn, which is a lovely, thick, pure wool DK in a huge range of colours. The fabric created is really dense and stands up on its own, so the button loop of this design does not need to fit over the handle of the mug.

Method

Using A and leaving a long end, cast on 20 sts.

Work 3 rows in garter stitch.

Now work in pattern.

Waffle pattern

Row 1 (RS): Using B, k1, *k1, sl1wyb; rep from * to last st, k1.

Row 2: Using B, k1, *sl1wyf, k1; rep from * to last st, k1.

Row 3: Using A, k1, *sl1wyb, k1; rep from * to last st, k1.

Row 4: Using A, k1, *k1, sl1wyf; rep from * to last st, k1.

These 4 rows set the pattern.

Cont in patt until work is almost long enough to fit round mug when slightly stretched, excluding handle.

Break off B.

Work 2 rows in garter stitch using A only.

Cast off, leaving a long end.

Button loop

Thread darning needle with a length of yarn A and use to make a button loop, beginning about ½in (1cm) below top edge and ending about 1½in (4cm) below top edge. Cover the loop with blanket stitch (see p.150). Attach button opposite button loop.

Making up

Thread the darning needle using the end of yarn left when casting on and join the first 2 stitches of the cast-on edge to the corresponding stitches on the cast-off edge. This will be the lower edge. Try hug on mug for placement of button and loop.

Cables make a lovely chunky fabric that holds the heat well, and are not difficult to work if you follow the instructions carefully. The double knitting yarn used is fabulous to work with and comes in a huge range of colours.

Sideways cable

Materials

Patons Fairytale Colour 4 Me DK 100% wool (98yd/90m per 50g)

Approx 35g in 4957 Aqua

A pair of 3.75mm (UK9:US5) needles

A pair of 4mm (UK8:US6) needles

Double-pointed needle (dpn) or cable needle (cn)

Small crochet hook

Darning needle for sewing up

Button

Size

3¼in (8cm) tall x any circumference (adjustable)

Tension

24 sts to 3¼in (8cm) in width measured over pattern on 4mm needles

Special techniques

Increasing (inc1): Knit into the front, then the back of the next st
Cable worked over 6 sts (C6F) (see instructions below)
Garter stitch (see p.138)

Pattern note

Do not press the finished work, as it will flatten the cables.

Cable over 6 sts (C6F)

Place next 3 sts on a double-pointed (dpn) or cable needle (cn) and leave at front of work. Knit next 3 sts, place the dpn or cn in position, then slide the 3 sts it holds towards the point and knit them. This is referred to as C6F. Return to main work and cont along the row.

Method

Using 3.75mm needles, cast on 20 sts, leaving a long end for sewing up.
Work 3 rows in garter stitch.
Change to 4mm needles.
Inc row: Inc1 in first st, p5, inc1, p6, inc1, p5, inc1. 24 sts.
The following 6 rows form the cable pattern and are repeated.
Row 1: Knit to end.
Row 2: K1, (p6, k2) twice, p6, k1.
Row 3 (cable row): K1, (C6F, k2) twice, C6F, k1.
Row 4: K1, (p6, k2) twice, p6, k1.
Row 5: Knit to end.
Row 6: K1, (p6, k2) twice, p6, k1.

Cont in patt until work is almost long enough to fit round the mug, excluding the handle.
Change to 3.75mm needles.
Work 4 rows in garter stitch.
Cast off along row, leaving last stitch on needle.

Make button loop

Insert crochet hook in stitch left on needle and work approx 16ch. Slip stitch into first stitch to form a loop. Fasten off, leaving a long end.

Making up

Thread the darning needle using the end of yarn left when casting on, and join first 2 stitches of the cast-on edge to corresponding stitches on the cast-off edge. This will be the lower edge of the hug. Darn in ends and attach button, checking fit if necessary.

The tab on this simple wrap-style hug is ideal if you want to make a feature of one beautiful button. The herringbone cable pattern is impressive, but is far easier to work than it looks.

Herringbone cable

Materials

Artesano Inca Cloud 100% alpaca (131yd/120m per 50g)

Approx 25g in 57 Fuchsia (used double throughout)

OR

Patons Sorbet chunky 73% cotton 27% acrylic
(82yd/75m per 50g)

Approx 25g in 5003 Coffee

A pair of 4.5mm (UK7:US7) needles

Button

Double-pointed needle (dpn) or cable needle (cn)

Size

3¼in (8cm) tall x any circumference (adjustable)

Tension

23 sts to approx 3¼in (8cm) in width measured over patt on 4.5mm needles

Special techniques

Increasing (inc1): Knit into the front, then the back of the next stitch
Decreasing (skpo and k2tog)
Cables (C4F and C4B) (see instructions)
Making a buttonhole (see instructions)

Pattern note

Cotton and cotton-mix yarns are not usually very stretchy. If you want to make this design for a mug with an irregular shape, choose a yarn that has some stretch, to accommodate any variations in diameter.

Method

Using a single strand of chunky yarn or two strands of Inca Cloud alpaca (see p51), cast on 7 sts.

Rows 1–2: Knit.
Row 3: Inc1, knit to last st, inc1. 9 sts.
Row 4: Knit.
Work buttonhole
Row 5: K3, cast off 3 sts, k to end.
Row 6: K3, cast on 3 sts over the sts cast off on the previous row, k3.
Rows 7–10: Knit.
Row 11: Inc1, k to last st, inc1. 11 sts.
Row 12: K1, p9, k1.
Row 13: Inc1, k9, inc1. 13 sts.
Row 14: K2, p9, k2.

Row 15: Inc1, k1, work cable (below) over next 9 sts, k1, inc1. 15 sts.

Cable pattern

Slip next 2 sts on to a dpn or cn and hold at back of work, k2, then k2 from dpn (C4B completed); k1; slip next 2 sts on to a dpn and hold at front of work, k2, then k2 from dpn (C4F completed).

Row 16: K3, p9, k3.
Row 17: Inc 1, k to last st, inc1. 17 sts.
Row 18: K4, p9, k4.
Row 19: K4, C4B, k1, C4F, k4.

Row 20: K4, p9, K4.
Row 21: Knit.

Rows 18–21 set the herringbone cable pattern. Rep them until work fits round mug between handles, ending with a WS row. Note that the shaping begins at the top and bottom of the handle.

Next row (dec): Skpo, knit to last 2 sts, k2tog. 15 sts.
Next row: Knit.
Next row: Skpo, knit to last 2 sts, k2tog. 13 sts.
Next row: Knit.

Next row: Skpo, knit to last 2 sts, k2tog. 11 sts.
Next row: Knit.
Next row: Skpo, knit to last 2 sts, k2tog. 9 sts.
Cast off.

Making up

Try the hug on the mug and attach button in correct position. Darn in any yarn ends.

A picot lower edge adds prettiness to this simple design in snug pure wool DK, while a length of fresh gingham ribbon threaded through eyelets adds a lovely extra touch.

Eyelets and ribbon

Materials

Patons Merino Wool DK 100% merino wool
(142yd/130m per 50g)

Approx 25g in 051 Denim

3.5mm (UK9–10:US4) needles for small size

4mm (UK8:US6) needles for medium size

4.5mm (UK7:US7) needles for large size

3.5mm (UK9:USE/4) crochet hook

Button (optional)

Darning needle for sewing up

Crochet hook (optional)

Approx 20in (50cm) narrow toning ribbon

Size

To fit mug approx 9[10:10½]in (23[25.5:27]cm) circumference excluding handle. Height is adjustable

Tension

22 sts to approx 4in (10cm) in width measured over stocking stitch on 4mm needles

Special techniques

Picot edge (see instructions)

Pattern note

If you don't think you can cope with knitting together stitches from the hem and cast-on edge to make the picot hem, just work row 7 as a normal purl row and sew up the hem later.

Method

Using 3.5mm[4mm:4.5mm] needles, cast on 49 sts.

Beg with a knit row, work 2 rows in st st.

Row 3: K2, *(yf, k2tog); rep from
* to last st, k1.

Row 4: K2, p to last 2 sts, k2.

Row 5: Knit.

Row 6: K2, p to last 2 sts, k2.

Form picot hem

Row 7: Knit together the next st and the corresponding st from the cast-on edge. Rep across row.

Rows 8–9: As rows 4–5.

Row 10 (WS): K2, p2, (yrn, p2tog, p1) to last 3 sts, p1, k2.

Rep rows 4–5 until sides reach the lower edge of the top of the handle. Work 4 rows in garter stitch.

Cast off, leaving a long end.

Note: If you wish to work a button loop, leave last st on needle and follow the instructions below. Check tension carefully.

Button loop (optional)

Insert crochet hook in st left on needle and work approx 15ch. Slip stitch into starting position to form a loop and fasten off.

Making up

Thread darning needle on the end of yarn left when casting on and join from lower edge of the hug to just under the handle of the mug, checking fit if necessary. Join top edges of hug and attach button to top corner to correspond with loop.

Thread ribbon through eyelets and tie in a bow at the front.

Ballet fans in your family will be sure to want one of these soft, frilly hugs.
You can make one in a single colour, or alternatively use up the smallest
oddments, changing colours as you like.

Tutu frilling

Materials

Any yarn in approx DK weight

Approx 20g in pink for plain version

Oddments in main (M) and contrast (C) for variation

A pair of 3.5mm (UK9–10:US4) needles for small size

A pair of 4mm (UK8:US6) needles for medium size

A pair of 4.5mm (UK7:US7) needles for large size

Darning needle for sewing up

2 buttons (optional)

2 small double-pointed needles for optional button loop

Size

To fit mug 4in (10cm) deep × 9[10:10½]in (23[25.5:26.5]cm)
circumference when slightly stretched

Making up

Thread the darning needle with the length of yarn left at cast-on and join edges of frill, matching rows carefully. Complete by adding a simple bar or a button loop (see below).

Simple bar

Try work on mug. Thread the darning needle with the length of yarn left when casting off and join upper corners by taking 2 to 3 strands loosely across top of the handle to form a short bar. Secure, then work over the strands in blanket stitch.

Button loop (optional)

Using a pair of double-pointed needles, cast on 3 sts and work in I-cord thus: k3 sts but do not turn. Pull yarn firmly across back of work and knit sts from right to left again. Rep until I-cord measures approx 2in (5cm). Fasten off and finish by making a loop with the I-cord and join to garter-stitch border of mug. Sew one button firmly over ends of loop. Attach the other button to the garter-stitch border on the opposite side.

Variation (See opposite)

Note: The example was made using an oddment of angora yarn in deep red for the frill and Patons Fairytale Colour 4 Me in 4954 Purple for the main part. It also includes a tab fastening (see instructions below).

Tension

22 sts to 4in (10cm) in width measured over stocking stitch on 4mm needles

Special techniques

Decreasing (skpo): Slip one stitch, knit one st, pass slipped st over
Making an I-cord (see p.148)

Method

Note: The example was made using an oddment of angora yarn in pink.

Cast on 90[96:100] sts using the correct size of needle, leaving a long end.
Work 4 rows in garter stitch.
Row 5: (Skpo) across row. 45[48:50] sts.
Row 6: Purl.
Row 7: Knit.
Row 8: Purl to last 2 sts, k2.
Rep last 2 rows until work reaches to the lower edge of top handle.
Work 4 rows garter stitch.
Cast off, leaving a long end.

Next row (buttonhole): K3, cast off 2 sts, work to end.

Next row: Knit, casting on 2 sts over sts cast off on previous row.

Knit 1 row.

Next row: Skpo, k to last 2 sts, k2tog. 6 sts.

Knit 1 row.

Cast off.

Making up

Join edges of frill, matching row ends carefully. Try work on mug. Attach button to correspond with tab.

Using C, cast on 90[96:100] sts, leaving a long end.

Work 4 rows in garter stitch.

Row 5: (Skpo) across row. 45[48:50] sts.

Row 6: Purl.

Change to M.

Row 7: Knit.

Row 8: Purl to last 2 sts, k2.

Rep last 2 rows until work reaches to the lower edge of top handle.

Work 4 rows garter stitch.

Cast off, leaving the last st on needle for tab.

Tab

Pick up and knit 14 sts (including first st) down one side of hug (excluding frill), turn.

Next row: Cast off 3 sts, work to end. 11 sts.

Next row: Cast off 3 sts, work to end. 8 sts.

Work 3 rows garter stitch.

A pretty pattern adds extra interest to this simple design, which is worked as a rectangle with an easy button loop. The pattern stitch looks equally good on either side, so just choose the one you like best.

Ears of corn

Materials

Patons Fairytale Colour 4 Me 100% wool (98yd/90m per 50g)

Approx 20g in 4952 Pale Green

A pair of 3.5mm (UK9–10:US4) needles for small mug

A pair of 4mm (UK8: US6) needles for medium mug

A pair of 4.5mm (UK7:US7) needles for large mug

Darning needle for sewing up

Button

Size

To fit mug 4in (10cm) deep x 9[10:10½]in (23[25.5:26.5]cm) circumference when slightly stretched

Note: As garter stitch is so stretchy, the same number of stitches can be used for the second and third sizes.

Tension

22 sts to 4in (10cm) in width measured over stocking stitch on 4mm needles

Special techniques

'Ears of corn' pattern (see method)

Pattern note

The stitch used is very stretchy, so this design will accommodate fairly wide variations in circumference.

Method

Using the correct needles for your chosen size of mug, cast on 48 sts and work 2 rows in k1, p1, rib.
Now work in pattern thus:

Row 1: K2, *p4, k2, yf, skpo; rep from * to last 6 sts, p4, k2.

Row 2: K6, *p2, yrn, p2tog, k4; rep from * to last 2 sts, k2.

Rows 3, 5 and 7: As row 1.

Rows 4, 6 and 8: As row 2.

Row 9: K4, yf, skpo, *p4, k2, yf, skpo; rep from * to last 2 sts, k2.

Row 10: K2, p2, yrn, p2tog, *k4, p2, yrn, p2tog; rep from *to last 2 sts, k2.

Rows 11, 13, and 15: As row 9.

Rows 12, 14 and 16: As row 10.

Rows 1–16 set pattern.

Rep rows 1–8 again.

K 1 row.

Cast off, leaving last st on needle.

Button loop

Cast on 15 sts, then cast them off again immediately.

Making up

Thread the darning needle using the end of yarn left when casting on, and join the last stitch to the corresponding stitch on the opposite edge of the hug. Attach the button, then try the hug on the mug and adjust loop length if necessary and sew in place.

Tip

For a taller mug, work rows 1–8 of the pattern again before the final cast-off row.

Random yarn in delicate pastel tones is perfect for this fresh, pretty design. The technique used to gather up the loose strands of yarn requires a little practice, but is very effective.

Butterflies

Materials

Patons Fairytale Colour 4 Me DK 100% wool
(98yd/90m per 50g)
Approx 20g in 4970 White/Lemon/Blue/Pink
A pair of 3.5mm (UK9–10:US4) needles for small mug
A pair of 4mm (UK8: US6) needles for medium mug
A pair of 4.5mm (UK7:US7) needles for large mug
Darning needle for sewing up
Button
Crochet hook (optional)

Size

To fit mug 4in (10cm) deep × 9[10:10½]in (23[25.5:26.5]cm)
circumference when slightly stretched

Tension

22 sts to 4in (10cm) in width measured over stocking stitch on 4mm needles

Special techniques

Butterfly stitch (see instructions)
Making a buttonhole (see instructions)
Decreasing (skpo and k2tog)
Sl5wfy: Slip 5sts with yarn at front of the work

Pattern notes

The stitch used is stretchy, so this design will accommodate fairly wide variations in circumference as well as irregularities in shape. For a taller mug, work rows 11–20 of the pattern again before final cast-off row.

Method

Note: When slipping stitches, do not strand yarn too tightly across front of work.

Using correct needles for your chosen size of hug, cast on 49 sts and work in pattern thus:

Butterfly stitch

Row 1 (RS): K2, * Sl5wyf, k5; rep from * ending last rep k2.
Rows 2, 4, 6 and 8: Purl.
Rows 3, 5, 7 and 9: As row 1.
Row 10 (WS): P4, *(insert right needle up through all 5 loose strands and transfer them to the left needle; purl through all the strands and the next st tog, p9), rep from * to end, ending last rep p4.
Note: The stitch that holds the loose strands will be at the centre of the slipped group.

Row 11 (RS): K7, * Sl5wyf, k5; rep from * ending last rep k7.
Rows 12, 14, 16 and 18: Purl.
Rows 13, 15, 17 and 19: As row 11.
Row 20 (WS): P9, *(insert right needle up through all 5 loose strands and transfer them to the left needle, then purl through all the strands and the next st tog, p9); rep from * to end.
These 20 rows set the patt.
Rep rows 1–10 again.
Cast off knit-wise, leaving last st on needle.

Edging and buttonhole tab

From the st left on needle, pick up and knit a further 14 sts down side of work.
Row 1: Cast off 3 sts, k to end. 11 sts.
Row 2: Cast off 3 sts, k to end. 8 sts.
Work 3 rows garter stitch.
Row 3–5: Knit.
Row 6 (buttonhole): K3, cast off 2 sts, k3.
Row 7: Knit, casting on 2 sts over sts cast off on previous row.
Row 8: Skpo, k to last 2 sts, k2tog. 9 sts.
Row 9: Knit.
Row 10: Skpo, k to last 2 sts, k2tog. 7 sts.
Cast off.

Button edge facing

With RS facing, rejoin yarn to opposite side of cover. Pick up and knit 14 sts evenly along side.
Knit 1 row.
Cast off, leaving a long end.

Making up

Press work lightly to flatten scalloped edge. Thread darning needle using the end of yarn left when casting on and join the last stitch to the corresponding stitch on the opposite edge. This will form the lower edge of the work. If you would prefer the button tab on the other side of the mug, join the cast-off edge instead. Try work on mug and attach button in correct position.
Note: The fastening for this design passes beneath the top of the mug handle.

Tip

You may find it easier to use a crochet hook to transfer the loose strands to the left needle before purling them together.

This design worked in garter stitch will stretch to fit almost any mug, and the simple base adds extra insulation. Two versions are given: plain and simple with no fastenings and stripes with an easy button loop.

First base

Materials

Patons Fairytale Colour 4 Me DK 100% wool (98yd/90m per 50g)

Version A (plain): 50g in 4958 Soft Pink

Version B (striped): Approx 20g each in 0051 White and 4989 Blue/Aqua/Green random

A pair of 4mm needles (UK8:US6)

Darning needle for sewing up

Crochet hook for button loop (optional)

Button (optional)

Size

To fit mug 4in (10cm) tall × 9[10:10½]in (23[25.5:26.5]cm) circumference when slightly stretched

Note: As garter stitch is so stretchy, the same number of stitches can be used for the second and third sizes.

Tension

22 sts to 4in (10cm) in width measured over garter stitch on 4mm needles
Use larger or smaller needles as required

Special techniques

Increasing (inc1): Increase by working into the front, then the back of the next stitch
Garter stitch (see p.138)

Method

Plain hug

Using 4mm needles, work in pink throughout.

Base

Cast on 8 sts, leaving a long end.
Row 1: Inc in each st by working into front, then back of stitch. 16 sts.
Row 2 and every alt row: K to end.
Row 3: *K1, inc1 by working into front, then back of st, rep from * to end of row. 24 sts.

Row 5: *K2, inc1; rep from * to end of row. 32 sts.
Row 7: *K3, inc1; rep from * to end of row. 40 sts.
Row 9: *K4, inc1; rep from * to end of row. 48 sts.

Second and third sizes only

Row 11: *K5, inc1; rep from * to end of row. 56 sts.
Work in garter stitch until the sides reach just to the top of the handle of the mug.
Cast off, leaving last st on needle if working a button loop, or a long end for sewing up.

Make button loop (optional)

Insert hook in stitch left on needle and use to crochet a chain loop OR form a double loop of yarn and finish by working over it using blanket stitch.

Striped hug

Using 4mm needles and white, cast on 8 sts and work base as for plain hug.
Next row (WS): Using white, knit to end of row.
Join in random yarn and work in stripe pattern (below) for sides.
Rows 1–2: Knit, using random yarn.
Rows 3–6: Knit, using white.
These 6 rows form patt. Rep until sides reach just to top of mug handle, carrying yarn not in use up side of work and ending after row 1 of patt.
Cast off loosely in random yarn, leaving

last st on needle to work button loop or a long end for sewing up.

Make button loop (optional)

Insert crochet hook in st left on needle and use to crochet a chain loop OR form a double loop of yarn and finish by working over it in buttonhole st.

Making up (both versions)

Thread darning needle using end of yarn left when casting on and join base seam, matching 'nubs' at end of garter stitch rows carefully. Join from lower edge of the cover to just below start of handle of mug, checking fit if necessary. Using the end of yarn left when casting on, join top edge of hug to fit over the handle of mug.

Tip

Cheat by working the hug in random yarn that produces instant stripes. Garter stitch is very stretchy so it will accommodate fairly wide variations in circumference as well as irregular shapes. If your mug has a very small circumference, end the base after row 7 and work the sides on 40 sts.

Rib stitch is ideal for mug hugs, as it will stretch to accommodate variations in circumference. The simple base provides extra insulation, random yarn adds interest and the button loop is worked in I-cord.

Random rib

Materials

Paton's Fairytale Colour 4 Me DK 100% wool
(98yd/90m per 50g)
Approx 25g in 4989 Blue/Aqua/Green mix
A pair of 4mm (UK8:US6) needles
Darning needle for sewing up

Size

To fit mug 4in (10cm) deep x 9[10:10½]in (23[25.5:26.5]cm)
circumference when slightly stretched

Tension

22 sts to 4in (10cm) in width measured over stocking stitch on 4mm needles

Special techniques

Increasing (inc1): Increase by working into the front, then the back of the next stitch

2 x 2 rib (see p.138)

Making an I-cord (see p.148)

Method

Base

With 4mm needles cast on 8 sts, leaving a long end.

Row 1: Inc1 by working into the front, then the back of every st. 16 sts.

Row 2 (and every alt row): K to end of row.

Row 3: *(K1, inc1 by working into the front, then the back of the next st); rep from * to end of row. 24 sts.

Row 5: *K2, inc1; rep from * to end of row. 32 sts.

Row 7: *K3, inc1; rep from * to end of row. 40 sts.

Row 9: *K4, inc1; rep from * to end of row. 48 sts.

Row 10: K2tog, k to last 2 sts, k2tog. 46 sts.

Second size only

Row 11: *K5, inc1; rep from * to end of row. 56 sts.

Row 12: K2tog, k to last 2 sts, k2tog. 54 sts.

Third size only

Row 11: *K5, inc1; rep from * to end of row. 56 sts.

Row 12: K to end of row.

Row 13: *K6, inc1; rep from * to end of row. 64 sts.

Row 14: K2tog, k to last 2 sts, k2tog. 62 sts.

All sizes: Cont in rib for sides.

Sides

Next row: (K2, p2) to last 2 sts, k2.

Next row: (P2, k2) to last 2 sts, p2.

These 2 rows set the 2 x 2 rib for sides. Cont in 2 x 2 rib until the sides reach just to the top of the handle of the mug.

Cast off, leaving last st on needle.

I-cord loop

From the st left on needle, pick up a further 2 sts close together. Make 15 rows of I-cord, k3tog, and fasten tail off into a loop.

Alternative loop

Transfer st from needle to a crochet hook and use to work approx 15ch. Slip st into same place to finish, then fasten off.

Making up

Thread darning needle with the end of yarn left when casting on. Join the base seam, matching ends of rows carefully. Join from the lower edge of the cover to just below the start of the handle of the mug, checking the fit if necessary. Attach button and adjust fit of loop before sewing in place.

> ### Tip
> The loop fastening of this mug can be placed on either side, depending on whether you cast off on a WS or RS row.

This pattern may look intricate, but in fact it's no more difficult to master than 2 x 2 rib. The 'mistake' is that the rib row is staggered to produce a lovely, thick, textured fabric.

Mistake rib

Materials

Patons Colour 4 Me DK 100% wool (98yd/90m per 50g)

Approx 30g in 4975 Walnut Brown

A pair of 4mm needles (UK8:US6)

A pair of 3.5mm (UK9–10:US4) double-pointed needles

Button

Darning needle for sewing up

Size

To fit mug 4in (10cm) deep x 9½[10:10½]in (24[25.5:26.5]cm) circumference when slightly stretched

Tension

20 sts to 4in (10cm) in width measured over rib patt on 4mm needles

Special techniques

Mistake rib (see instructions)
Increasing (inc1): Increase by working into the front, then the back of the next stitch
Making an I-cord (see p.148)

Pattern notes

The rib pattern is very stretchy, so this mug hug will accommodate fairly wide variations in circumference. It will also expand or contract to accommodate irregular shapes. Any DK-weight yarn may be substituted for the yarn used in the example.

Method

Base

Using 4mm needles, cast on 8 sts, leaving a long end.

Row 1: Inc in each st by working into the front, then the back of the st. 16 sts.

Row 2 (and every alt row): Purl to end of row.

Row 3: *K1, inc1 by working into the front, then the back of the next st; rep from * to end of row. 24 sts.

Row 5: *K2, inc1; rep from * to end of row. 32 sts.

Row 7: *K3, inc1; rep from * to end of row. 40 sts.

Second and third sizes only

Row 9: *K4, inc1; rep from * to end of row. 48 sts.

Third size only

Row 11: *K5, inc1; rep from * to end of row. 56 sts.

All sizes

Next row: Inc in first st, p to end of row. 41[49:57] sts.

Now cont in rib patt for sides.

Mistake rib

Pattern row: *K2, p2; rep from * to last st, k1.

This single row forms patt. Rep until sides are long enough to reach to top handle of mug, ending on a WS row. Cast off in rib patt, leaving an end of approx 1yd (1m) for I-cord.

Making up

Thread darning needle using the end of yarn left when casting on and join base, matching rows carefully. Join first rows of rib to just below handle of mug. Thread the long end of yarn on to a darning needle and weave it down to approx 1in (2.5cm) below the top edge of the hug.

I-cord loop

With 3.5mm needles pick up 3 stitches very close together, ending approx 1in (2.5cm) below top edge of the hug. Use the woven-down end of yarn to work an I-cord approx 2in (5cm) long. Thread yarn through end of I-cord and catch stitches neatly to edge of hug, approx 1in (2.5cm) below the start point. Try on mug and attach a button to correspond with I-cord loop.

This easy 4-row pattern makes a thick, textured design that is perfect either with or without a base. It's easy to vary the size simply by changing the needles, and a beautiful button with two fastening loops adds a special touch.

Daisy stitch

Materials

Pure wool double knitting to Aran-weight yarn

Approx 25g Orange

A pair of 3.5mm (UK9–10:US4) needles for small mug

A pair of 4mm (UK8: US6) needles for medium mug (shown)

A pair of 4.5mm (UK7:US7) needles for large mug

Darning needle for sewing up

3.5mm (UK9:USE/4) crochet hook

Large button

Size

To fit mug 9[10:10½]in (23[25.5:26.5]cm) in circumference when slightly stretched

Tension

Approx 22 sts to 4in (10cm) in width measured over pattern on 3.5mm needles

Approx 20 sts to 4in (10cm) in width measured over pattern on 4mm needles

Approx 18 sts to 4in (10cm) in width measured over pattern on 4.5mm needles

Note: Use larger or smaller needles to obtain correct tension

Special techniques

Yarn round needle (yrn): Wrap yarn completely round needle

Increasing (inc1): Increase by working into the front, then the back of the next stitch

Mattress stitch (see p.146)

Double crochet (dc) (see p.147)

Pattern notes

This design features two loops that fasten over a single button, or two buttons if you prefer. It may also be made without a base. To do this, cast on 49 sts and work in pattern (see below). The pattern lies flat, so no additional edging will be needed.

Method

Base

Using 3.5[4:4.5]mm needles cast on 8 sts, leaving a long end.

Row 1: Inc by working into the front, then the back of every st. 16 sts.

Row 2 and every alt row: K to end of row.

Row 3: *(K1, inc1 by working into the front, then the back of the st); rep from * to end of row. 24 sts.

Row 5: *K3, inc1; rep from * to end of row. 30 sts.

Row 7: *K4 inc1; rep from * to end of row. 36 sts.

Row 9: *K5, inc1; rep from * to end of row. 42 sts.

Row 11: *K6, inc1; rep from * to end of row. 48 sts.

Row 12: Inc1, purl to end. 49 sts.

Now work in pattern for sides.

Pattern

Row 1 (RS): Knit to end.

Row 2: K1, *p3tog, yrn, purl same 3 sts tog again, k1; rep from * to end of row.

Row 3: Knit to end.

Row 4: K1, p1, k1, *p3tog, yrn, purl same 3 sts tog again, k1; rep from * to last 2 sts, p1, k1.

These 4 rows form pattern.

Cont in patt until sides reach to about ½in (1cm) below top of mug, ending with RS facing.

Cast off knit-wise, but do not fasten off the final loop.

Button loops

Insert crochet hook in final loop, work *18ch, ss into base of 18ch to create first button loop. Work 6dc down side of hug, then rep from * again. Cont in dc to end of pattern section. Fasten off.

Making up

Press work lightly, following instructions on ball band. Thread darning needle on end of yarn left when casting on, and join base using mattress stitch as far as first pattern row. Sew in ends. Attach a single large button to the top corner of the hug opposite the button loops. Slip cover over mug and fasten by slipping lower button loop over button first, followed by top button loop.

Working the sides in cables adds a luxurious touch as well as extra insulating properties. Two different cable patterns have been used for the two different yarns, so just choose the one you prefer.

Cream and coffee

Materials

Cream: Patons Wool blend Aran 63% new wool 37% acrylic (202yd/185m per 50g)
Approx 25g in 002 Cream
Coffee: Artesano Inca Cloud Alpaca 100% alpaca (121m per 50g)
Approx 20g in 004 Oatmeal
A pair of 3.75mm (UK9:US5) needles for Cream hug
A pair of 4mm (UK8:US6) needles for Coffee hug
Cable needle (cn) or double-pointed needle (dpn)

3.5mm (UK9:USE/4) crochet hook for button loop (optional)
Button (optional)
Darning needle for sewing up

Size

To fit mug circumference 9[10:10½]in (23[25.5:26.5]cm)

Tension

24 sts to 4in (10cm) in width measured over cable pattern on 3.75mm needles for Cream hug or 4mm needles for Coffee hug

Special techniques

Reversed stocking stitch (rev st st)
Cables (C4F): Place 2 sts on a cable needle and hold at front of work, k2, then k sts from cable needle)
Increasing (inc1): Increase by working into front, then the back of next stitch

Pattern note

Either variation may be worked without a base if you prefer. To do this, cast on the appropriate number of stitches for the required size and work a foundation of 2 rows of k1, p1 rib before beginning the cable pattern.

Method

Cream *(See left)*

*Cast on 8 sts leaving a long end for sewing up and work base thus:
Row 1: Inc in each st. 16 sts.
Row 2 (and every alt row): Purl.
Row 3: (K1, inc1) to end. 24 sts.
Row 5: (K2, inc1) to end. 32 sts.
Row 7: (K3, inc1) to end. 40 sts.
Row 9: (K4, inc1) to end.* 48 sts.

Second size only

Row 11: (K5, inc1) to end of row. 56 sts.

Third size only

Row 13: (K6, inc1) to end of row.
64 sts.

All sizes

Begin cable and rev st st patt on row
10[12:14] so base is also presented in
rev st st:

Cream cable pattern

Row 1: P2, (k4, p4) to last 6 sts, k4, p2.

Row 2: K2, (p4, k4) to last 6 sts, p4, k2.

Row 3: P2, (C4F, p4) to last 6 sts, C4F,
p2.

Row 4: As row 2.

These 4 rows form patt. Rep until work
is long enough to reach to the top of
the handle of the mug.

Cast off knit-wise, leaving a long end
for sewing up.

Making up

Thread darning needle on the end of
yarn left when casting on and join the
base, matching stitches carefully. Join first
stitches of cable pattern to just below
handle of mug. Use cast-off end to
crochet a chain button loop or join top
of the cast-off edge together as shown.

Coffee *(See page 87)*

Work first 9 rows of base as for Cream
from * to *. 48 sts.

Now follow the instructions below for
size variations.

First size

Row 10: Inc1, p to last st, inc1. 50 sts.

Second size

Row 10: Purl.

Row 11: (K5, inc1) to end.
56 sts.

Row 12: Purl.

Third size

Row 10: Purl.

Row 11: (K5, inc1) to end. 56 sts.

Row 12: Purl.

Row 13: (K6, inc1) to end. 64 sts.

Row 14: P2 tog, p to last 2 sts, p2tog.
62 sts.

Now foll patt to work the sides on
these 50[56:62] sts thus:

Coffee cable pattern

Row 1: P2, *(k4, p2); rep from * to
end of row

Row 2: K2, *(p4, k2); rep from * to
end of row.

Row 3 (cable): P2, *(C4F, p2); rep
from * to end.

Row 4: As row 2.

Row 5: As row 1.

Row 6: As row 2.

These 6 rows form the cable patt. for
Coffee. Rep until work is long enough
to reach to top of handle of mug,
ending on a WS row.

Cast off in patt, leaving last st on
needle.

Button loop

Place crochet hook in last stitch and
use to work approx 14ch. Slip stitch
into first chain to form a button loop.
Fasten off.

Making up

Complete as for Cream, adding a
button to correspond to button loop.

Tip

*Any cable pattern works
well over this design, but if
you want to substitute a different
pattern make sure you check the
stitch count carefully.*

This delicate lacy pattern will turn the most basic mug into a thing of beauty. Use different shades of blue, purple or even pink to suggest the myriad tones of bluebells in nature.

Bluebells

Materials

Berocco Pure Merino DK 100% merino wool
(126yd/115m per 50g ball)
Approx 20g in 4585 Peacoat
A pair of 3.5mm (UK9–10:US4) needles for small mug
A pair of 4mm (UK8:US6) needles for medium mug
A pair of 4.5mm (UK7:US7) needles for large mug
Darning needle for sewing up
Medium button

Size

To fit mug approx 9[10:10½]in (23[25.5:26.5]cm)
in circumference
Note: If your mug is very tall, work extra pattern rows to make it deeper (see note below pattern instructions). An extra 6 rows will increase the depth by about ¾in (2cm).

Tension

22 sts to 4in (10cm) in width measured over stocking stitch on 4mm needles

Special techniques

Lace pattern (see instructions)
Decreasing (skpo): Slip one stitch, knit one st, pass slipped st over
Increasing (inc1): Increase by working into the front, then the back of the next stitch

Pattern notes

The lace fabric used for this design will stretch to accommodate almost any shape of mug. The pattern is a little tricky, so you will need to pay close attention to your work, but to make things easier, the size of the finished hug can be varied simply by using larger or smaller needles.

Method

Using 3.5mm[4mm:4.5mm] needles, cast on 8 sts, leaving a long end.
Row 1: Inc in every st. 16 sts.
Rows 2, 4, 6, 8 and 10: Purl to end of row.
Row 3: *K1, inc1 by working into the front, then the back of the stitch, rep from * to end of row. 24 sts.
Row 5: *K2, inc1; rep from * to end of row. 32 sts.
Row 7: *K3, inc1; rep from * to end of row. 40 sts.

Row 9: *K4, inc1; rep from * to end of row. 48 sts.
Row 11: *K5, inc1; rep from * to end of row. 56 sts.
Row 12: Purl to end, dec 1 at end of row. 55 sts.
Now work in pattern with a 2-st garter-stitch border at each side.

Lace pattern

Row 1 (WS): K2, p3, *k3, p3; rep from * to last 2 sts, k2.
Row 2: K5, *p2tog, yrn, p1, k3; rep from * to last 2 sts, k2.
Row 3: As row 1.
Row 4: K5, *p1, yrn, p2tog, k3; rep from * to last 2 sts, k2.
Row 5: As row 1.
Row 6: K3, k2tog, *(p1, yrn) twice, p1, (sl1, k2tog, psso); rep from * to last 8 sts, (p1, yrn) twice, skpo, k3.
Row 7: K5, *p3, k3; rep from * to last 2 sts, k2.
Row 8: K2, p1, yrn, p2tog, *k3, p1, yrn, p2tog; rep from * to last 2 sts, k2.
Row 9: As row 7.
Row 10: K2, p2tog, yrn, p1, *k3, p2tog, yrn, p1; rep from * to last 2 sts, k2.
Row 11: As row 7.
Row 12: K2, p2, yrn, p1, *(sl1, k2tog, psso), (p1, yrn) twice, p1; rep from * to last 2 sts, k2.
These 12 rows form the patt.
Rep the 12 patt rows once, ending with RS facing for next row.

Note: For a taller mug, work rows 1–6 again at this point.
Next row: (K1, p1) to last st, k1.
Next row: (P1, k1) to last st, p1.
Work 3 further rows in 1x1 rib, ending with WS facing for cast-off.
Cast off in rib, leaving last stitch on needle, turn.

Button loop

Cast on 16 sts to form button loop, then cast them off immediately.

Making up

Thread length of yarn left after casting on and join base using mattress stitch. Join free end of button loop neatly to cast-on point. Attach button to opposite side.

This design looks really impressive, but it's actually fairly easy to work as only one colour is used at a time. Ring the changes to use up scraps of yarn; it also looks effective in heather tones.

Tulips

Materials

Patons Fairytale Colour 4 Me DK 100% wool (98yd/90m per 50g)

Hug with base: Approx 20g yellow (A)

Oddments of dark green (B) and red (C)

Hug without base: Approx 15g red (A)

Oddments of dark green (B) and yellow (C)

A pair of 3.75mm (UK9:US5) needles for small and medium sizes

A pair of 4mm (UK8:US6) needles for large size

Button for each design

Size

To fit mug 4in (10cm) deep × 9[10:10½]in (23[25.5:26.5]cm) circumference when slightly stretched

Tension

22 sts to 4in (10cm) in width measured over stocking stitch on 4mm needles

Special abbreviations

Sl1(3)wyf: Slip 1 (3) st(s) with yarn at the front of the work

Sl1(3)wyb: Slip 1 (3) sts with yarn at the back of the work

MK (make knot): K3, turn, p1, p2tog, turn, k2tog

Increasing (inc1): Increase by working into the front, then the back of the next stitch

Pattern notes

The pattern is worked by creating loops to represent leaves, then a knot of contrast yarn is worked into the top of each to represent a flower head. The technique for spreading the loops across the front of the work is rather like cabling; if you find it easier, a cable needle may be used.

Method

Hug with base

Base

Using 3.75mm[3.75mm:4mm] needles and A, cast on 8 sts, leaving a long end.

Row 1: Inc in each st. 16 sts.

Rows 2, 4, 6 and 8: P to end of row.

Row 3: *K1, inc1; rep from * to end of row. 24 sts.

Row 5: *K2, inc1; rep from * to end of row. 32 sts.

Row 7: *K3, inc1; rep from * to end of row. 40 sts.

Row 9: *K4, inc1; rep from * to end of row. 48 sts.

First size only

Row 10: P to last st, p2tog. 47 sts.

Second and third sizes only

Row 10: Purl to end of row. 48 sts.

Row 11: *K5, inc1; rep from * to end of row. 56 sts.

Row 12: Purl to last st, inc1. 57 sts.

All sizes

Still using A, cont in patt for sides. (47[57:57]) sts.

Pattern

Row 1: Using A, knit to end.

Row 2: K2, p to last 2 sts, k2.

Join in B.

Row 3: Using B, knit.

Row 4: Using B, k7; *k3 wrapping yarn round needle 3 times for each st, k7; rep from * to end.

Break off B.

Change to A.

Row 5: Using A, K3, *sl1wyb, k3, sl3wyb and dropping the extra wraps, k3; rep from * to last 4 sts, sl1, k3.

Row 6: K2, p1, *sl1wyf, p3, sl3wyf, p3; rep from * to last 4 sts, sl1wyf, p1, k2.

Row 7: K7, *sl3wyb, k7; rep from *, ending k7.

Row 8: K2, p5, *sl3wyf, p7; rep from * to last 7 sts, p5, k2.

Row 9: K5, *sl2wyb, drop next (B) st off needle at front of work, sl the 2 slipped sts back to LH needle, pick up and knit the dropped st, k3 (including the central B st); drop next (B) st off needle at front of work, k2, pick up and knit the dropped st, k3; rep from * to last 2 sts, k2.

Row 10: Sl first 5 sts; join in C and * [(p1, k1, p1) in next st, sl2wyf)] twice; (p1, k1, p1) in next st**; sl3wyf; rep from * to last 5 sts, ending last rep at **, sl last 5 sts.

Row 11: Sl first 5 sts; using C, *MK in next 3 sts, (sl2wyb, MK) twice**; sl3wyb; rep from * ending last rep at **, sl last 5 sts.

Break off C.

Row 12: Using A, k2, purl to last 2 sts, k2.

Row 13: Using A, knit to end.

Row 14: K2, p to last 2 sts, k2.

Rep rows 13–14 until work measures 2in (5cm) from row 4 (yarn B).

Join in C and rep rows 13–14 once more.

Break off C.

Join in B and work 3 rows k2, p2 rib.

Cast off, leaving last st on needle.

Button loop

Insert crochet hook into last st on needle and use to crochet a chain loop, or work a button loop using blanket stitch over 2 strands of yarn.

Making up

Join base as far as garter stitch row in B, matching row ends carefully. Darn in yarn ends. Attach button to correspond with loop.

Hug without base

Using 3.75mm[3.75mm:4mm] needles and A, cast on 47[57:57] sts.

Work 3 rows k1, p1 rib.

Next row: K2, p to last 2 sts, k2.

All sizes

Foll rows 1–14 of patt for hug with base.

Now rep rows 13 and 14 until work measures 2¾in (7cm) from cast-on row.

Using A, work 3 rows k1, p1 rib.
Cast off in rib.
Work button loop as for hug with base.

Making up

Join rib at bottom of hug, matching rows carefully. Attach button. Darn in ends.

The stripes used for this design represent all the colours of the rainbow, so they are a wonderful way to cheer up the most miserable day, and of course an excellent way to use up oddments of yarn.

Rainbow

Materials

Paton's Fairytale Colour 4 Me DK 100% wool (98yd/90m per 50g)

Approx 10g each of Red, Orange, Yellow, Green, Blue, Indigo (Dark Blue) and Violet

A pair of 3.75mm needles (UK9:US5) for small size

A pair of 4mm needles (UK8:US6) for medium size

A pair of 4.5mm needles (UK7:US7) for large size

Darning needle for sewing up

Button

Size

To fit mug 9[10:10½]in (23[25.5:26.5]cm) in circumference when slightly stretched

Tension

22 sts to 4in (10cm) in width measured over stocking stitch on 4mm needles

Special techniques

Sl1p-wise wyb: Slip 1 stitch as if to purl, with yarn at the back of work
Increasing (inc1): Increase by working into the front, then the back of the next stitch
Making an I-cord (see p.148)

Pattern note

This design is an excellent way to use up really short lengths of yarn: each stripe (2 rows of pattern) may be worked with around 1yd (1m) of yarn. Don't forget that there will be lots of ends to sew in!

Method

Base

Using 3.75mm[4mm:4.5mm] needles, cast on 8 sts, leaving a long end of yarn.

Row 1: Inc in each st by working into front, then back of stitch. 16 sts.

Row 2 (and every alt row): P to end of row.

Row 3: *K1, inc1 by working into front, then back of stitch; rep from * to end of row. 24 sts.

Row 5: *K2, inc1; rep from * to end of row. 32 sts.

Row 7: *K3, inc1; rep from * to end of row. 40 sts.

Row 9: *K4, inc1; rep from * to end of row. 48 sts.

Row 11: *K5, inc1; rep from * to end of row. 56 sts.

Row 12: P to last st, inc. 57 sts.

Now work in patt for sides.

Pattern

Row 1: Using red, *(k3, sl1p-wise wyb); rep from * to last st, k1.

Row 2: K1, *(yf, sl1p-wise, yb, k3); rep from * to end.

Row 3: Using orange, k1, *(sl1p-wise wyb, k3); rep from * to end.

Row 4: *(K3, yf, sl1p-wise, yb); rep from * to last st, k1.

These four rows set the patt.

Rep these rows, changing colour every 2 rows in the sequence red, orange, yellow, green, blue, indigo and violet until work reaches to just below handle of mug, ending after a RS row.

Next row: Cast off, leaving last loop on needle.

Button loop

From the loop left on needle, pick up a further 2 sts from top corner of work. Work in I-cord on these sts for approx 2½in (6cm).
Fasten off, leaving a long end.

Alternative button loop

From the loop left on the needle, use a crochet hook to work approx 15ch. Finish with a ss into the first st. Fasten off.

Making up

Join the base and the first 2 rows of the pattern, matching row ends carefully. Sew in all yarn ends. Join the end of I-cord loop to where stitches were picked up. Attach button to opposite top corner.

Smocked ribbing adds interest to this design in wonderfully soft alpaca DK. The method of tying stitches together is a bit tricky, but it is well worth the effort to produce such a stylish hug.

Culture smock

Materials

Artesano 100% alpaca DK (109yds/100m per 50g)

Approx 25g in SFN21 Biscuit

A pair of 3.5mm needles (UK9:US4) for small size

A pair of 4mm needles (UK8:US6) for medium size

A pair of 4.5mm needles (UK7:US7) for large size

Double-pointed needle (dpn) or cable needle (cn)

Darning needle for sewing up

Button

Size

3½in (9cm) deep x any circumference (adjustable)

Tension

22 sts to 4in (10cm) in width measured over stocking stitch on 4mm needles

Special techniques

Tied stitches (see instructions)
Ribbing (see instructions)
Increasing (inc1): Increase by working into the front, then the back of the next stitch
Mattress stitch (see p.146)
Making an I-cord (see p.148)

Pattern note

If you do not feel confident about working the tie stitch, work the hug in rib omitting the tie stitch rows.
At making-up stage, catch the relevant stitches together by oversewing two or three times, just as if smocking a sewn garment.

Method

Base (optional)

With 3.75[4:4.5]mm needles, cast on 8 sts, leaving a long end.

Row 1: Inc in each st by working into the front, then the back of the stitch. 16 sts.

Rows 2, 4, 6, 8, 10 and 12: Purl.

Row 3: *K1, inc1 by working into the front, then the back of the st, rep from * to end of row. 24 sts.

Row 5: *K2, inc1; rep from * to end of row. 32 sts.

Row 7: *K3, inc1; rep from * to end of row. 40 sts.

Row 9: *K4, inc1; rep from * to end of row. 48 sts.

Row 11: *K5, inc1; rep from * to end of row. 56 sts.

Row 13: *K6, inc1; rep from * to end of row. 64 sts.

Row 14: Purl, inc1 at each end. 66 sts.

Sides

Row 1: (K2, p2) to last 2 sts, k2.

Row 2: (P2, k2) to last 2 sts, k2.

Work 2 further rows in rib as set.

Next row (tie): (Rib 10, work tie over next 6 sts) to last 2 sts, p2.

Working the tie

Slip next 6 sts on to a dpn or cn and hold at front of work. Wrap the yarn twice anti-clockwise round these 6 sts. Pull tight to secure sts, then work off 6 sts as k2, p2, k2. Cont in rib to next tie. Work 5 rows rib.

Next row (tie): (Rib 2, work tie over next 6 sts) to last 10 sts, rib 10.

Work 5 rows rib.

Cont as set, working tie on 6th and 12th foll rib rows.

Work 5 rows rib.

Cast off in rib, leaving last st on needle. Join base using mattress st.

Beg with st left on needle, pick up and knit a total of 17 sts down one side of hug, then 17 sts down other side of hug.

Cast off.

Button loop

Join yarn to edge of hug, approx 1in (2.5cm) from top. Pick up 3 sts very close together from edge, and work in I-cord on these 3 sts for approx 2¼in (5.5cm).

Fasten off.

Making up

Attach free end of loop to side of hug, approx ¾in (2cm) below start of loop. Attach button to opposite side. Darn in yarn ends.

For a really special touch, it's easy to add initials to your hug. This simple design is worked upwards without a base, and the chart gives an easy-to-work version of every letter of the alphabet.

Getting personal

Materials

Patons Fairytale Colour 4 Me DK 100% wool (98yd/90m per 50g)

Approx 20g in chosen shade

Oddment of black for initial

A pair of 4mm (UK8:US6) needles

Darning needle for sewing up

3.5mm (UK9:USE/4) crochet hook

Button

Size

3½in (9cm) deep x 9[10:10½]in (23[25.5:26.5]cm) circumference

Tension

22 sts to 4in (10cm) in width measured over stocking stitch on 4mm needles

Special techniques

1 x 1 rib (see p.138)
Intarsia (see p.144)
Chain stitch (see p.147)

Pattern notes

The featured yarn is ideal for this design: it is slightly thicker than some DK yarns and produces a firm, dense fabric. Wind off small balls of yarn before beginning the intarsia section to avoid carrying stitches over the back of motif. Twist yarns together firmly when changing colour to prevent holes.

Method

Cast on 48[54:56] sts, leaving a long end for sewing up.
Work 4 rows 1 x 1 rib.
Next row: Knit.

Tip

If your intarsia looks uneven, go over each stitch using the darning needle to ease them gently into shape.

Next row: K2, p to last 2 sts, k2.
Rep last 2 rows once.
Next row: K8[9:10] sts. Work chosen initial from chart over next 6 sts.
This last row sets position of chart.
Cont in stocking st and intarsia with 2-st garter-stitch edging at sides, working chart as set.
Work 3 rows stocking stitch, then work 3 rows rib.
Cast off in rib, leaving last st on needle.

Button loop

Insert crochet hook in loop left on needle and use to crochet approx 14ch for loop. Take back through work at base of first chain and fasten off.

Making up

Press lightly. Thread darning needle using end of yarn left when casting on and join the lower ribbed edge to corresponding stitches on the cast-off edge. Attach button to correspond with loop, adjusting position to ensure a good fit. Darn in yarn ends.

Chart of alphabet letters

Each square = 1 st and 1 row

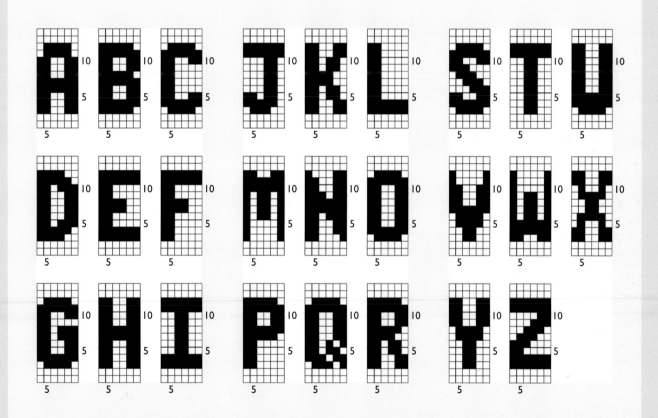

Show someone how much you care by adding a heart to your hug in simple intarsia – but if you're worried about working from a chart, the instructions are written out in full. The size can be varied just by changing needle size.

With love

Materials

Patons Fairytale Colour 4 Me 100% wool (98yd/90m per 50g)

Approx 25g in 4985 New Lime (M)

Oddment of 4967 Red (C)

A pair of 3.5mm (UK9–10:US4) needles for small size

A pair of 4mm (UK8:US6) needles for medium size

A pair of 4.5mm (UK7:US7) needles for large size

Darning needle for sewing up

Size

To fit mug 9[10:10½]in (23[25.5:26.5]cm) in circumference

Tension

22 sts to 4in (10cm) in width measured over stocking stitch on 4mm needles

Special techniques

Intarsia (see p.144)

Pattern notes

The recommended yarn is a pure wool DK that washes well and is available in a wide range of shades. It is slightly thicker than some DK yarns, so it is ideal for working intarsia designs. Do not carry the yarn over the back of the heart as it may pull it out of shape; work the second main colour section using a small separate ball of yarn. If your mug has a circumference of less than 9in (23cm), end base after row 9 and work the sides on 42 sts.

Method

All sizes

Using M and 3.5mm[4mm:4.5mm] needles cast on 8 sts, leaving a long end for sewing up.

Row 1: Inc in each st by working into front, then back of the stitch. 16 sts.

Row 2 and every alt row: Purl to end of row.

Row 3: *K1, inc1 by working into front, then back of st; rep from * to end of row. 24 sts.

Row 5: *K2, inc1; rep from * to end of row. 30 sts.

Row 7: *K3, inc1; rep from * to end of row. 36 sts.

Row 9: *K4, inc1; rep from * to end of row. 42 sts.

Row 11: *K5, inc1; rep from * to end of row. 48 sts.

Row 12: Purl to end.

**Work 4 rows in stocking st.
Work heart from chart over 11 sts and 14 rows, setting the first contrast st on the 12th st of row OR follow instructions on panel to work heart without using the chart.

Work 3 rows in stocking st (adjust height here if required).

Work 3 rows in k1, p1 rib.

Join in C and cast off sts along top of hug knit-wise, leaving final st on needle.

Button loop

Cast on 18 sts, then cast them off immediately. Fasten off, leaving a long end.

Working the heart without a chart

Row 1: K11 sts in M, k1 in C, using small separate ball of M, k to end.

Row 2: K2, purl until 13 sts rem on left needle, p3C, using M, purl to last 2 sts, k2.

Row 3: K9M, k5C, using M, k to end.

Row 4: K2, purl to last 15 sts, p7C, using M, purl to last 2 sts, k2.

Row 5: K8M, k7C, using M, k to end.

Row 6: K2, purl to last 16 sts, p9C, using M, purl to last 2 sts, k2.

Row 7: K7M, k9C, k to end.

Row 8: K2, purl to last 17 sts, p11C, using M, purl to last 2 sts, k2.

Row 9: K6M, k11C, k to end.

Row 10: As row 8.

Row 11: As row 9.

Row 12: As row 8.

Row 13: K7M, k4C, k1M, k4C, using M, k to end.

Row 14: K2, purl to last 15 sts, p2C, p3M, p2C, using M, purl to last 2 sts, k2.

Variation

For a hug without a base, cast on 48 sts and work 2 rows k1, p1 rib for the lower edge. Then work the instructions for the hug with base from **. When making up, join the first 2 rows of rib to sit below mug handle.

Making up

Join base of hug at first 2 rows. Sew free end of button loop to where first stitch was cast on. Attach button to opposite top corner.

Note: If your mug has a circumference of less than 9in (23cm), end base after row 9 and work the sides on 42 sts.

Heart chart
Each square = 1 st and 1 row

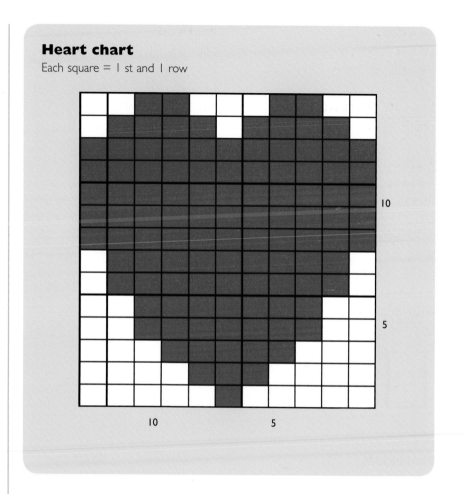

The simplest of intarsia pattern charts can be used to add a cute llama to your hug. Vary the colour of the llama and the background shades used to make a different creature for every member of the family.

Llama

Materials

Twilley's Freedom Spirit DK 100% wool
(120yds/110m per 50g ball)
Approx 15g in 517 Brown Mix (A)
Standard DK yarn
Approx 15g blue (B)
Oddment of white or natural (C)
A pair of 4mm (UK9:US5) needles
3.5mm (UK9:USE/4) crochet hook (optional)
Darning needle for sewing up
Button (optional)

Size

3¼in (8cm) deep x 9[10:10½]in (23[25.5:26.5]cm)
circumference (adjustable)

Tension

22 sts rows to 4in (10cm) measured over pattern on 4mm needles

Special techniques

Intarsia (see p.144)

Pattern notes

Two stitches are cast off after the foundation rib to form a narrow bar beneath the mug handle. This helps to keep the design square and prevent distortion of the motif. Wind off small balls of each of the yarns before beginning the intarsia pattern, and do not carry across the back of the work.

Method

Using A, cast on 53[55:57] sts, leaving a long end for sewing up.
Work 2 rows in garter stitch.

Next row: Cast off 2 sts, k3[4:5] sts, work across row 1 of chart to set position of llama, knit to end. 51[53:55] sts.

Next row: Purl, working row 2 of chart pattern as set and working last 2 sts as k2 to form a narrow garter-stitch edge.

Cont in stocking stitch, working llama from chart and keeping first 2 sts of every row in garter stitch, until chart is complete.

Next row: Using A, work 1 row in stocking stitch (adjust height here if required).

Work 2 rows in garter stitch as for lower edge.

Cast off, leaving long end of yarn.

Making up

Using an oddment of brown or black yarn, embroider an eye on the llama. Thread darning needle using the end of yarn left when casting on and join the first two rows of rib to form a small bar at the lower edge of the hug. Try the hug on the mug and take the remaining length of yarn across the top of the handle two or three times to form a narrow bar then finish with blanket stitch. Alternatively, add a button loop by using the yarn end to crochet approx 15ch and slip stitch to form a loop. Attach button and darn in yarn ends.

Tip

If your intarsia looks uneven, use the point of the darning needle to ease the stitches gently into place.

Llama chart

Each square = 1 st and 1 row

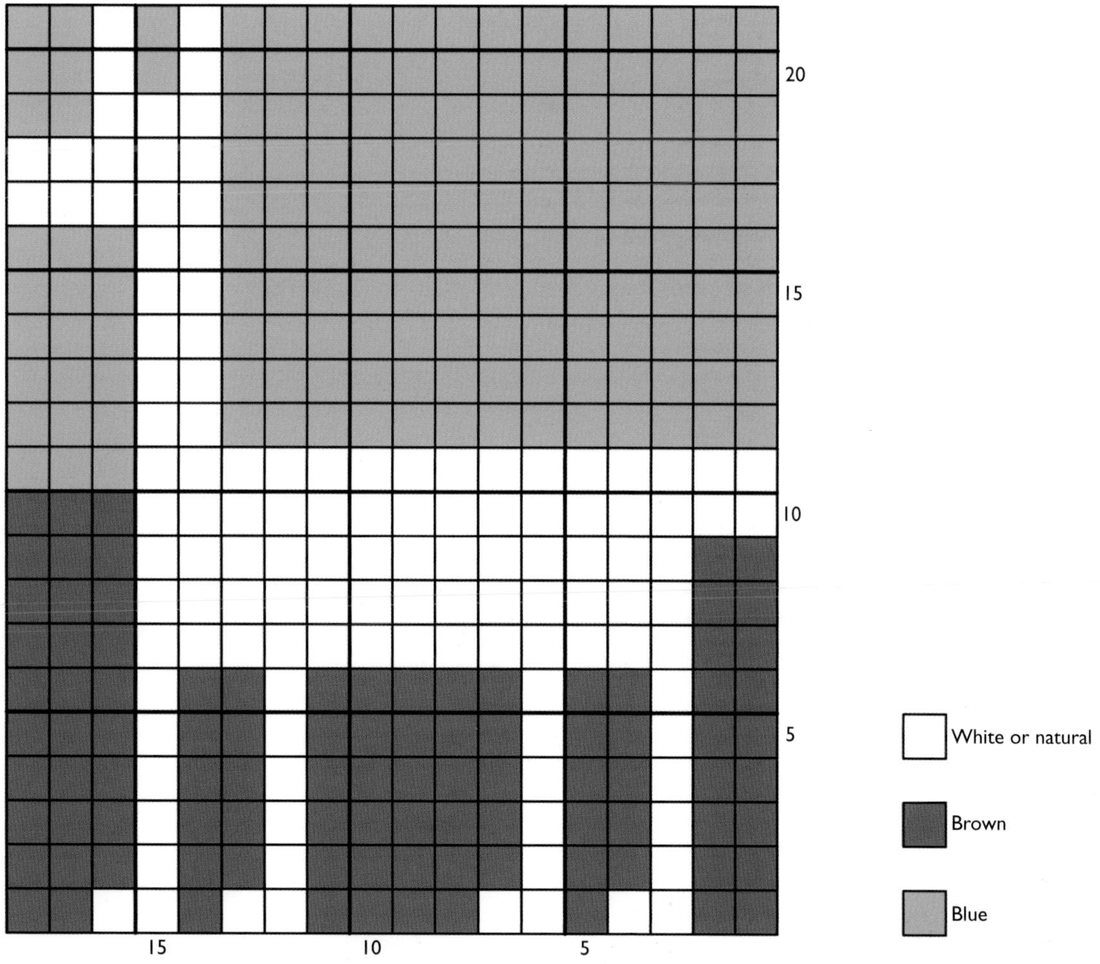

20

15

10

5

White or natural

Brown

Blue

15   10   5

This design is shaped to fit a typical latte mug that flares out from a narrow base to a wider top. The smaller size fits a standard mug, while the larger one is designed for a real monster!

Regular or grande?

Materials

Regular: Sirdar Tweedie chunky 45% acrylic 40% wool 15% alpaca (100m per 50g)
Approx 30g in 285 Cedar
Grande: Patons Eco Wool Chunky 100% untreated new wool (80m per 50g)
Approx 35g in 1727 Brown/Gold/Cream
A pair of 4.5mm (UK7:US7) needles
A pair of 5mm (UK6:US8) needles
Darning needle for sewing up
Button or toggle

Size

Regular: To fit a mug with a base diameter of approx 2½in (6cm) and a top diameter of 3½in (9cm). The example shown is about 4¾in (12cm) tall
Grande: To fit a mug with a base diameter of approx 2¾in (7cm) and a top diameter of 4in (10cm). The example shown is about 6in (15cm) tall

Tension

16 sts to 4in (10cm) in width measured over stocking stitch on 5mm needles.

Special techniques

Increasing (inc1): Increase by working into the front, then the back of the next stitch

Pattern notes

The sides of this design are shaped by increasing at intervals as the work grows. If the size of your mug falls between the two examples given, work increases to 44 sts and add a few rows of stocking stitch to increase the height, then work the button loop and border as given. The fastening can be made to go over or under the handle, according to preference – see photographed examples above.

Method

Regular

Using 4.5mm needles, cast on 32 sts and knit 2 rows to form the garter-stitch edge. Change to 5mm needles.

Next row: Knit to end.

Next row: K2, p to last 2 sts, k2.
Rep last 2 rows once.

Next row (inc): K5, inc, (k6, inc) × 3, k5. 36 sts.

Keeping the 2-st garter-stitch border correct, work 7 rows in stocking stitch.

Next row: K7, inc, (k6, inc) × 3, k7. 40 sts.

Work 7 rows in stocking stitch.

Button loop

Next row: Cast on 14 sts at beg of row, the cast them off immediately and knit to end

Work 3 rows garter stitch.

Cast off loosely.

Grande

Using 4.5mm needles, cast on 36 sts and knit 2 rows to form the garter-stitch edge.

Change to 5mm needles.

Next row: Knit to end.

Next row: K2, p to last 2 sts, k2.
Rep last 2 rows once.

Next row (inc): K7, inc1, (k6, inc1) × 3, k7. 40 sts.

Keeping the 2-st garter-stitch border correct, work 7 rows in st st.

Next row: K8, inc1, (k7, inc1) × 3, k7. 44 sts.

Work 7 rows in st st.

Next row: K8, inc1, (k8, inc1) × 3, k8. 48 sts.

Work approx 5 rows in stocking stitch or length required to take sides of hug to just below handle.

Work 3 rows garter stitch.

Cast off, leaving last stitch on needle.

Button loop

Insert crochet hook in stitch left on needle and work a chain long enough to reach over handle of mug.

Making up

Join ends of lower border. Attach end of buttonhole loop neatly to side border about ½in (1cm) below start of loop, or slip stitch into first stitch of crochet chain and fasten off. Attach button or toggle to opposite side. A second decorative button if required.

This simple design could not be easier to knit – it's just a stocking-stitch rectangle worked sideways, then felted for extra thickness. A blanket-stitch edging and easy chain-stitch heart add the finishing touches.

Felted

Materials

Coats Wash+Filz-it! Felting Wool 100% wool (55yd/50m per 50g)

Approx 25g in 19 Red

Oddment of standard DK in black

A pair of 5mm (UK6:US8) needles

Button

Darning needle with a sharp point for sewing up

Size

3¼in (8cm) deep x any circumference (adjustable)

Tension

18 sts to 4in (10cm) in width measured over stocking stitch on 5mm needles *before* felting

Special techniques

Felting (see instructions)
Blanket stitch (see p.148)

Pattern notes

Take care to slip the first stitch of every row when knitting the rectangle, as this helps to prevent the edge from becoming too thick after felting. Sew in all yarn ends before felting the work.

Method

Using 5mm needles, cast on 11 sts.
Row 1: Sl1, k to end.
Row 2: Sl1, p to end.
Rep these 2 rows until work is just over 1in (2.5cm) longer than the mug circumference, excluding handle.

Felting

Darn in yarn ends. Place work in a net bag in drum of washing machine. Add a small amount of detergent and a heavy item or two, such as a towel or a pair of jeans, to help the felting process. Run through a full 104°F (40°C) cycle.

Remove from drum and pull carefully to shape: you may have to ease the edges apart if they have curled. Check the length carefully and adjust by pulling work evenly if necessary.

Making up

Press work under a damp cloth until really flat. Work a neat row of blanket stitch round all edges. Work a fastening loop approximately in the centre of one of the shorter sides and cover with small blanket stitches. Using a neat chain stitch, add an open heart motif to the front of the hug.

Tip

If you do not feel confident about working a heart freehand, draw one on to your felted fabric with tailors' chalk and use as a guide for embroidery. Alternatively, just add a ready-made iron-on or sew-on motif.

If your takeaway has cost a packet, you won't want your fingers burned a second time! This snug sleeve fits any size disposable cup from monster macchiato to little latte, protecting fingers and keeping coffee warm.

Big bucks

Materials

Creative Poems Self-Striping Aran 100% wool
(109yd/100m per 50g)
50g in 001 (Blue/Brown/Pink) knits all three sleeves
A pair of 3.75mm (UK9:US5)
A pair of 4mm (UK8:US6) needles
Darning needle for sewing up

Size

To fit a small[medium:large] 10[16:20]fl oz (296[473:592]ml) disposable drinks cup, as supplied by all major chains
Note: The small and medium sizes can also be used for larger cups if you prefer a sleeve rather than a full cover.

Tension

20 sts to 4in (10cm) measured over stocking stitch using 4mm needles

Special techniques

Felting (optional) (see instructions)
Mattress stitch (see p.146)

Method

For all sizes

Using 3.75mm needles, cast on 46 sts.

Row 1: K1, p1 to end.

This row sets the 1 x 1 rib. Rep 3 [5:7] times.

Change to 4mm needles.

Work in stocking stitch for 4[6:8] rows.

Next row (first inc): K6, *(inc1 st, k7); rep from * to end. 51 sts.

Cont straight in stocking stitch for a further 5[7:9] rows.

Small size only

Work 5 rows in 1 x 1 rib.

Cast off in rib leaving a long end.

Medium size only

Next row (second inc): K6, *(inc1 st, k8); rep from * to end. 56 sts.

Cont straight in stocking stitch for a further 7 rows.

Work 7 rows in 1 x 1 rib.

Cast off in rib, leaving a long end.

Large size only

Next row (second inc): K6, *(inc1 st, k8); rep from * to end. 56 sts.

Cont straight in stocking stitch for a further 9 rows.

Next row (third inc): K6, *(inc1, k9); rep from * to end. 61 sts.
Cont straight in stocking st for a further 2 rows or to required height.
Work 7 rows in 1 x 1 rib.
Cast off in rib, leaving a long end for sewing up.

Making up

Thread darning needle on to end of yarn left when casting off and use mattress stitch to join the edges neatly.

Felting

The featured yarn can be felted slightly. To do this, run the hug through a machine cycle at 86°F (30°C) with a little washing powder and an old towel. Stretch over a spare cup and allow to dry, remembering that work will shrink slightly in height when felted.

Note: The medium- and large-size photographed examples have been felted, while the smallest sleeve shows the unfelted yarn.

A naked mug!

Techniques

How to make your mug snug

Measurements

Measure your mug before you begin. A standard mug is about 4in (10cm) high but diameter may vary. For simple mug hugs worked sideways, this diameter is not important. For mug hugs that are worked from the bottom upwards, different sizes are given.

Use a tape measure to measure the diameter of your mug. Remember that knitting is stretchy, so if your mug falls between two sizes then the smaller one is probably best. If your mug is an unusual shape, measure mid-way between its widest and narrowest parts, and use a stitch with plenty of stretch, such as garter stitch.

Tension

Just a small difference can have a noticeable effect on the size of the finished piece. Tension swatches are boring, but well worth the effort. They need not be wasted: label them and file them for future reference.

Working a swatch

To work a tension swatch, cast on at least 24 stitches using your chosen yarn and needles. Work for about 30 rows until you have produced a piece that is roughly square, then cast off. Press lightly, following instructions on the ball band. Lay the swatch flat and measure carefully across the central section to check that your stitch count matches that of the pattern.

Materials and equipment

Needles

The designs in this book are worked on straight needles. Your work will be small, so choose short needles. Most needles are metal, though larger sizes may be plastic. Some knitters like bamboo because it is warm to the touch. Use whichever you prefer, making sure they have smooth points and are not bent.

Double-pointed needles

These are straight needles with a point on both ends. They are usually fairly short, so you could even work your mug hug using them. Wind an elastic band round one end to prevent stitches falling off. They are also used to work I-cord button loops.

Cable needle

These are useful for holding stitches when you work cables, but not essential. A double-pointed needle can be used just as effectively.

Yarn

Any yarn can be used for your mug hug and it's a great way to use up oddments. Wool or alpaca provide good insulation, but choose pre-shrunk or superwash yarn or it will shrink when you wash it. Cotton or cotton-mix yarn is also excellent.

Thickness of yarn

In theory, any thickness of yarn can be used, but fine yarns will not provide such good insulation. Yarns that are too bulky may swamp the mug, especially if the pattern chosen has a lot of texture. Finer yarns can be used double to produce a thicker knitted fabric. Check tension if you plan to do this.

To begin with, it's best to choose double knitting yarn, worked to a tension of about 6 stitches and 8 rows to 1in (2.5cm) over stocking stitch, or chunky yarn worked to a tension of 4 to 5 stitches per inch.

Substituting yarn

Take a strand of yarn and wind it closely, in a single layer, round a flat metal or wooden rule. Count the number of 'wraps' formed along 1in (2.5cm) of the rule. This figure is the number of wraps per inch produced by the yarn. Refer to the chart below to check whether the yarn is a suitable substitute.

yarn type	tension in sts per 4in (10cm)	tension in sts per in (2.5cm)	use yarn with this number of wraps per in (2.5cm)
4-ply	30	7.5	15–16
4-ply/DK	28	7	14–15
DK/Aran	26	6.5	13–14
Aran/chunky	24	6	12–13
Chunky	22	5.5	11–12

Knitting techniques

Simple cast-on

  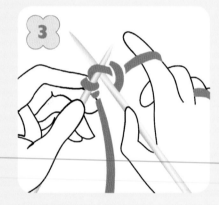

1 First, form a slip knot on the left needle. Insert the right needle into the loop and wrap yarn round it as shown.

2 Pull the yarn through the first loop to create a new one.

3 Slide the new loop on to the left needle.

There are now 2 stitches on the left needle. Continue in this way until you have the required number of stitches.

Cable cast-on

For a firmer edge, cast on the first 2 stitches as shown above. When casting on the third and subsequent stitches, insert needle between cast-on stitches on left needle, wrap yarn round and pull through to create a loop (1). Slide loop on to left needle. Repeat to end of row (2).

Thumb method cast-on

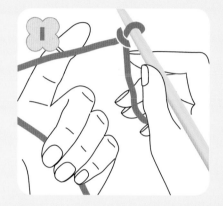  

1 Make a slip knot some way from the end of the yarn and place on the needle. Pull the knot tight.

2 Hold the needle in right hand and wrap the loose tail end round the left thumb, from front to back. Push the needle point through the thumb loop from front to back. Wind the ball end of yarn round needle from left to right.

3 Pull the loop through thumb loop, then remove thumb. Gently pull the new loop tight, using the tail yarn. Repeat until the desired number of stitches are on the needle.

Knit stitch

1 Hold the needle with the cast-on stitches in your left hand. Place the tip of the empty right needle into the first stitch and wrap the yarn round as for casting on.

2 Slip the newly-made stitch on to the right needle.

3 Pull the yarn through to create a new loop.

Continue in the same way for each stitch on the left-hand needle.

To start a new row, turn the work to swap the needles and repeat steps.

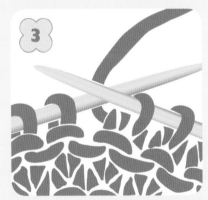

Purl stitch

1 Hold the yarn at the front of the work as shown.

2 Place the right needle into the first stitch from front to back. Wrap the yarn round the needle in an anti-clockwise direction as shown.

3 Bring the needle back through the stitch and pull through.

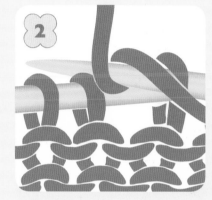

A Garter stitch

Knit every row.

B Stocking stitch

Knit on RS rows and purl on WS rows.

C Moss stitch

With an even number of stitches:
Row 1: (K1, p1) to end.
Row 2: (P1, k1) to end.
Rep rows 1 and 2 for pattern.

With an odd number of stitches:
Row 1: * K1, p1; rep from * to last stitch, k1.
Rep to form pattern.

D Single (1 x 1) rib

With an even number of stitches:
Row 1: *K1, p1; rep from * to end.
Rep for each row.

With an odd number of stitches:
Row 1: *K1, p1, rep from * to last stitch, k1.
Row 2: *P1, k1, rep from * to last stitch, p1.

E Double (2 x 2) rib

Over a multiply of 4 sts stitches:
Row 1: *K2, p2; rep from * to end.
Rep for each row.

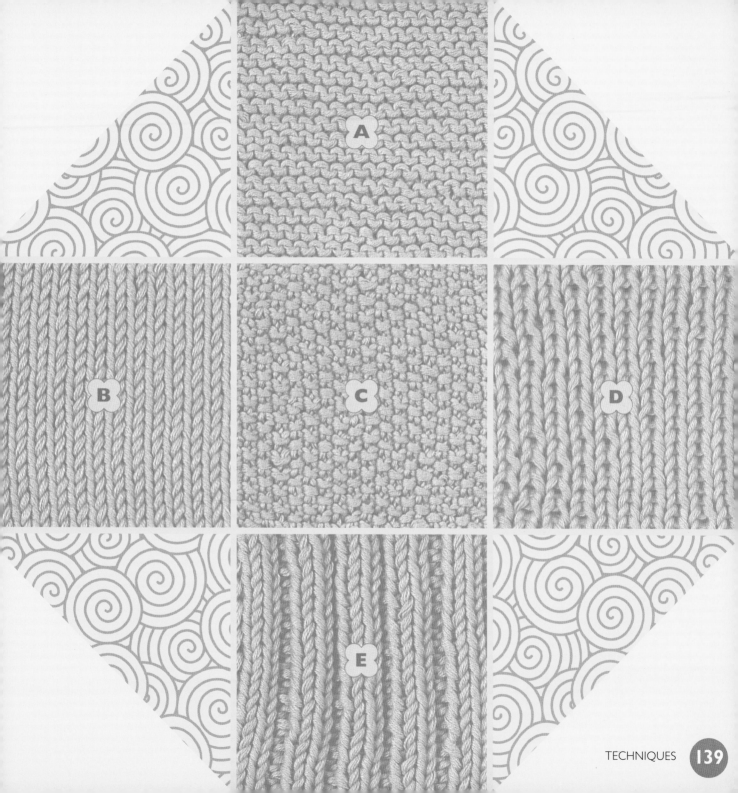

Cable stitch

With the help of a cable needle, these decorative stitches are quite straightforward. Stitches are slipped on to the needle and then knitted later to create the twists.

Front cable worked over 4 stitches (C4f)

1 Slip the next 2 sts on to a cable needle and hold in front of work.

2 Knit the next 2 sts from the left needle as normal, then knit the 2 sts from the cable needle.

Back cable worked over 4 sts (C4b)

Slip the next 2 sts on to a cable needle and hold at back of work.

Knit the next 2 sts from the left needle as normal, then knit the 2 sts from the cable needle.

Bases

Adding a base is really easy. It provides extra insulation and also saves using a separate drip mat. Garter stitch and stocking stitch variations are given, each worked in eight sections to increase by 8 stitches for every two rows. Use the garter-stitch base for finer yarn and the stocking-stitch base with DK or thicker yarn for a less-bulky base.

Calculating base size

To calculate how many stitches you need, work a tension swatch in your chosen pattern. This is important because some patterns, especially cables, 'pull in' the work widthways. Measure around the lower edge of the mug beneath the handle and multiply by the number of stitches per inch (or centimetre) in the tension swatch. For example, if the mug is 10in (25.5cm) round its base and the tension 6 sts to 1in (2.5cm), you will need 60 sts. Subtract a few stitches for the width of the handle. In this case, a 56-stitch base should work perfectly.

Edge stitches

Some patterns (especially lace) may curl at the sides unless you work one or two edge stitches in garter stitch on every row. Take care to include these in your calculations.

Repeat patterns

The number of stitches may be adjusted slightly to accommodate a repeat pattern, and one or two either way will not make your work too big or too small. For example, if a pattern repeats over 4 sts, make sure the number of stitches cast on will divide by 4. Adjust by increasing or decreasing on the final row of the base.

Odd-shaped mugs

If your mug is an irregular shape, don't worry. All you need to do is measure mid-way between its widest and narrowest parts to work out how many stitches to cast on, and choose a stretchy fabric such as garter stitch, rib or lace pattern. A button and loop can be added halfway up to prevent sides gaping.

Adjusting tension

Tension can easily be adjusted by using larger or smaller needles. Some of the designs may be made for mugs of different sizes by changing needles to produce more or fewer stitches to the inch or centimetre.

How many stitches will I need?

The table below is an approximate guide – one or two stitches either way should not matter. If in doubt, go lower: knitting usually stretches to accommodate slight variations.

Sizing guide						
Yarn	**4-ply**	**Aran**	**DK (light)**	**DK (standard)**	**Chunky**	
Sts to 4in (10cm)	28	26	24	22	20	18
Sts to 1in (2.5cm)	7	6.5	6	5.5	5	4.5
9in mug (actual sts)	68	65	58	53	48	44
Base size (no of sts)	64	64 (− 2) = 62	56	48 (+ 2) = 50	48 (− 2) = 46	40 (+ 2) = 42
10in (25cm) mug (actual sts)	70	65	60	55	50	45
Base size (no of sts)	64 + 2 = 66	64 (− 2) = 62	56	48 (+ 2) = 50	48 (− 2) = 46	40 (+ 2) = 42
10½in (26cm) mug (actual sts)	73.5	68	63	58	52	47
Base size (no of sts)	72 (− 2) = 70	64	56 (+ 2) = 58	56 (− 2) = 54	48	40 + 4 = 44

Key to sizing guide

In base size (+) or (−) suggests a no of sts to inc/dec on final row of base to achieve a good fit.

Stocking-stitch base

For thicker yarns, a stocking-stitch base is usually the best choice.

Method

Cast on 8 stitches.

Row 1: Inc by working into the front and back of every stitch. 16 sts.

Row 2 and every alt row: Purl all stitches.

Row 3: (K1, inc1) to end. 24 sts.
Row 5: (K2, inc1) to end. 32 sts.
Row 7: (K3, inc1) to end. 40 sts.
Row 9: (K4, inc1) to end. 48 sts.
Row 11: (K5, inc1) to end. 56 sts.
Row 13: (K6, inc1) to end. 64 sts.
Row 15: (K7, inc1) to end. 72 sts.

Work increases until you have enough stitches to fit round the mug base.

Final row: Purl to end, inc/dec if necessary to achieve desired no of sts. Now work straight in chosen stitch until sides reach the height you require.

Garter-stitch base

This base method is ideal for yarns up to DK weight and any size of mug – just work increases until there are enough stitches to fit round its circumference when slightly stretched. If necessary, increase or decrease stitches on final row (see chart), then work straight on the stitches in your chosen pattern for the sides. The base is joined into a circle when the work is finished.

Method

Cast on 8 sts.

Row 1: Inc by working into front and back of every stitch. 16 sts.

Row 2 and every alternate row: Knit all stitches.

Row 3: (K1, inc1) to end. 24 sts.
Row 5: (K2, inc1) to end. 32 sts.
Row 7: (K3, inc1) to end. 40 sts.
Row 9: (K4, inc1) to end. 48 sts.
Row 11: (K5, inc1) to end. 56 sts.
Row 13: (K6, inc1) to end. 64 sts.
Row 15: (K7, inc1) to end. 72 sts.

Work incs until there are enough sts to fit around the base.

Final row: Knit to end, inc/dec if necessary.

Colour knitting

Intarsia designs

These are designs worked using blocks of colour. Where several colours are used you can combine Fair Isle and intarsia techniques by dropping some colours and carrying others.

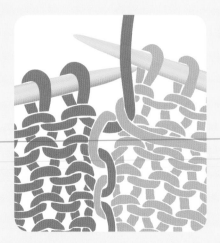

Use a separate ball of yarn for each block, and twist the yarns together each time you change colour to prevent holes forming between the blocks. Remember not to pull the yarns too tightly across the back of the work.

Reading charts

Most charts are shown in squares, with a square representing one stitch. Charts are usually marked in increments of 5 or 10 stitches to make counting easier.

Stocking stitch

When working in stocking stitch on straight needles, read the chart from right to left on knit (RS) rows and from left to right on purl (WS) rows. Check carefully after every purl row to make sure the pattern stitches are in the correct position.

Finishing off

Casting off

1 Knit 2 sts on to the right needle, then slip the first st over the second st and let it drop off the needle (1 st remains).

2 Knit another st so you have 2 sts on the right needle again.

Repeat the process until there is only 1 st on the left needle. Break yarn and thread through remaining st.

Casting off in rib

To cast off in rib, keep pattern of rib by working sts as knit or purl as appropriate and at the same time cast off in the normal way.

Sewing up

Mattress stitch

Place the pieces to be joined on a flat surface laid together side-by-side with right sides towards you. Using matching yarn, thread a needle back and forth with small, straight stitches. The stitches form a ladder between the two pieces of fabric, creating a flat, secure seam. This technique is usually known as mattress stitch.

Stocking stitch joins

The edges of stocking stitch tend to curl, so it may be tricky to join. The best way to join it is to use mattress stitch to pick up the bars between the columns of stitches.

Working upwards or downwards according to preference, secure the yarn to one of the pieces you want to join. Place the edges of the work together and pick up a bar from one side, then pick up the corresponding bar from the opposite side. Repeat. After a few stitches, pull gently on the yarn and the two sides will come together in a seam that is almost invisible. Take care to stay in the same column all the way. Do not pull the stitches tight at first, as you will not be able to see what you are doing.

Crochet techniques

Chain stitch (ch)

1 With hook in right hand and yarn resting over middle finger of left hand, pull yarn taut. Take hook under, then over yarn.

2 Pull the hook and yarn through the loop while holding slip knot steady. Rep to form a foundation row of chain stitch (ch).

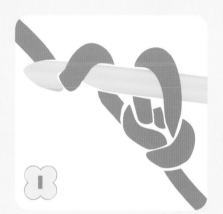

Double crochet (dc)

1 Place hook into a st. Wrap yarn round hook and draw the loop back through the work towards you.

2 There should now be two loops on the hook. Wrap yarn round hook again, then draw through both loops, leaving one loop on the hook (one double crochet [dc] now complete). Rep to continue row.

Fastenings

Knitted loops

There's a really simple way to make a button loop: cast on an appropriate number of stitches where you want the loop, then cast them off immediately (see Simply Snug, page 10). This method is ideal because the loop created is quite stretchy and is easy to adjust. For hugs worked sideways, knitted-in loops can be made either when casting on or casting off. For hugs worked upwards, make the knitted-in loop either just before you cast off or at the end of casting off, depending on which side of your work you want the loop to appear.

Keeping it simple

The simplest way to fasten your hug is not to fasten it at all. Most of the patterns in this book will stretch enough to go over the handle of a mug, so you can simply sew stitches together at the top and bottom.

Chain loops

If you prefer a finer loop or decide to add a loop later, a crochet chain works well. Choose a hook size slightly smaller than the needles used for the main knitting, and work a chain of an appropriate length. Slip stitch into the first chain to finish, or fasten off and sew in the end of the loop.

I-cord loops

Using a pair of double-pointed needles (one to hold the stitches and the other to work them) cast on or pick up an even number of stitches. For a button loop, three stitches are ideal. Knit across the stitches, but do not turn the work. Pull the yarn tight across the back of the stitches and knit them again. Carry on in this way until the I-cord is long enough to make a loop. Break yarn leaving a long end and run it through all 3 stitches to fasten off.

Blanket-stitch loops

If you've forgotten to knit in loops, are scared of I-cord and can't crochet, don't despair. Form a double strand of yarn into a loop in the appropriate position, then blanket stitch neatly over it (see page 150).

Buttons

Gorgeous buttons can make a very simple hug look fantastic, so take care when choosing them. Medium or large sizes are best, as small ones may slip out of the button loops. Toggles also make excellent fastenings.

Pins, badges and brooches

If you would rather not sew on a button, then don't – use a pin instead! Good haberdashery stores sell pretty pins, or use a favourite badge or even a brooch. Work a button loop in the normal way and slip this over the pin, or work a simple tab by picking up a few stitches at the side of your work and knitting a few rows.

Finishing touches

Blanket stitch

Work from left to right. The twisted edge should lie on the outer edge of the fabric to form a raised line. Bring needle up at point A, down at B and up at C with thread looped under the needle. Pull through. Take care to tighten the stitches equally. Repeat to the right. Fasten the last loop by taking a small stitch along the lower line.

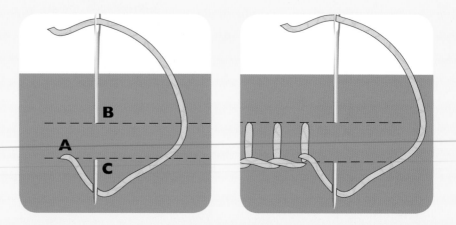

Abbreviations

approx	approximately		**mm**	millimetres
beg	beginning		**p**	purl
ch	chain		**patt**	pattern
cont	continue		**p2tog**	purl two stitches together
cm	centimetres		**p-wise**	with needles positioned as for a purl stitch
cn	cable needle			
dec	decrease		**rem**	remaining
dc	double crochet		**rep**	repeat
DK	double knitting		**RS**	right side of work
dpn	double-pointed needle		**rev st st**	reverse stocking stitch
foll	following		**skpo**	slip one, knit one, pass slipped stitch over
inc	increase by working into front, then back of stitch		**ss**	slip stitch
in	inch(es)		**st(s)**	stitch(es)
k	knit		**st st**	stocking stitch
k-wise	with needles positioned as for working a knit stitch		**tbl**	through the back of the loop
k2tog	knit two stitches together		**tog**	together
m	metre(s)		*	work instructions following * then repeat as directed

Conversions

Needle sizes

UK	Metric	US
14	2mm	0
13	2.5mm	1
12	2.75mm	2
11	3mm	–
10	3.25mm	3
–	3.5mm	4
9	3.75mm	5
8	4mm	6
7	4.5mm	7
6	5mm	8
5	5.5mm	9
4	6mm	10
3	6.5mm	10.5
2	7mm	10.5
1	7.5mm	11
0	8mm	11
00	9mm	13
000	10mm	15

UK/US yarn weights

UK	US
2-ply	Lace
3-ply	Fingering
4-ply	Sport
Double knitting	Light worsted
Aran	Fisherman/worsted
Chunky	Bulky
Super chunky	Extra bulky

About the author

Alison Howard has been knitting since she was nine, when her grandmother taught her how to make a scarf for her teddy. Over the years she has mastered most of the major techniques and produced many successful creations, though the knitted bikini was not among them.

Knitting remained an enjoyable hobby during many changes of career, though she never imagined that it would help her to earn a living. Spells in journalism, public relations and marketing followed a degree in English, as she tried to find a way to earn an honest crust while doing something she actually liked. Then a tiny ad in the local paper caught her eye and she applied for a job editing craft books.

She now works mainly as a freelance editor in the craft sector. She also edits various pieces of academic writing and occasionally helps to teach English to university students of various nationalities. This book seemed a natural progression from editing and contributing to various knitting titles for GMC Publications.

**For Colonel Chester Ignatius Finbarr St. John Phillips,
who always likes to help with a spot of knitting.**

Index

Names of patterns are given in italics.

To place an order, or to request a catalogue, contact:

GMC Publications Ltd

Castle Place, 166 High Street, Lewes, East Sussex, BN7 1XU

United Kingdom

Tel: +44 (0)1273 488005   **Fax:** +44 (0)1273 402866

Website: www.gmcbooks.com

Orders by credit card are accepted